Retirement Security in the Great Recession

Few events have posed as many challenges for retirement and retirement policy as the crisis of the late 2000s. At the end of the last decade, the United States experienced the Great Recession—a combination of unprecedented wealth losses and historically high unemployment increases that marked the longest economic recession since the Great Depression. These adverse economic shocks coincided with the burgeoning entry into retirement by the baby boomer generation, those born in the United States between 1946 and 1964. The confluence of these trends meant that retirees may have faced greater economic insecurity than at any point since World War II.

This book brings together a number of influential researchers whose work is focused on economic policies and their impacts on retirement income security. They come from both academic and policy backgrounds. Specifically, half of the eight contributors are academics, while the other four come from think tanks in Washington, DC. This book is thus intended to combine research and policy.

This book was published as a special issue of the *Journal of Aging and Social Policy*.

Christian E. Weller, PhD, is an associate professor of public policy at the McCormack Graduate School of Policy Studies at the University of Massachusetts Boston. He is also a senior fellow at the Center for American Progress in Washington, DC. Professor Weller's research interests and expertise include pensions, Social Security, macroeconomics, and international finance. Professor Weller has published more than 100 academic and popular articles in addition to more than 200 policy reports and short policy commentaries. He is frequently cited in the press.

Retirement Security in the Great Recession

Edited by
Christian E. Weller

Routledge
Taylor & Francis Group

LONDON AND NEW YORK

First published 2011
by Routledge
2 Park Square, Milton Park, Abingdon, Oxon, OX14 4RN

Simultaneously published in the USA and Canada
by Routledge
270 Madison Avenue, New York, NY 10016

Routledge is an imprint of the Taylor & Francis Group, an informa business

This book is a reproduction of the *Journal of Aging and Social Policy*, vol.22, issue 2. The Publisher requests to those authors who may be citing this book to state, also, the bibliographical details of the special issue on which the book was based

Typeset in Times New Roman by Taylor & Francis
Printed and bound in Great Britain by CPI Antony Rowe, Chippenham, Wiltshire

British Library Cataloguing in Publication Data
A catalogue record for this book is available from the British Library

ISBN13: 978-0-415-58903-1

Disclaimer
The publisher accepts responsibility for any inconsistencies that may have arisen in the course of preparing this volume for print.

Contents

Introduction: Retirement Security in the Great Recession

CHRISTIAN E. WELLER, PhD

Associate Professor, Department of Public Policy and Public Affairs, McCormack Graduate School of Policy Studies, University of Massachusetts Boston, Boston, Massachusetts, USA, and Senior Fellow, Center for American Progress, Washington, DC, USA

Few events have posed as many challenges for retirement and retirement policy as the crisis of the late 2000s. At the end of the last decade, the United States experienced the Great Recession—a combination of unprecedented wealth losses and historically high unemployment increases that marked the longest economic recession since the Great Depression. These adverse economic shocks coincided with the burgeoning entry into retirement by the baby boomer generation, those born in the United States between 1946 and 1964. The con uence of these trends meant that retirees may have faced greater economic insecurity than at any point since World War II.

The public has shown an appetite for policy reform to increase retirement security. Poll after public opinion poll has indicated that respondents were either as worried about their retirement as they were about health care or even more worried about retirement than health care. The crisis only exacerbated the public's desire for more policy intervention to stabilize their retirement wealth and thus provide some sense of certainty for retirees.

Christian E. Weller, PhD, is an associate professor of public policy at the McCormack Graduate School of Policy Studies at the University of Massachusetts Boston. He is also a senior fellow at the Center for American Progress in Washington, DC. Professor Weller's research interests and expertise include pensions, Social Security, macroeconomics, and international nance. In 2006, he was awarded the Labor and Employment Relations Association's Outstanding Scholar-Practitioner Award. He is also an institute fellow with the Gerontology Institute at the University of Massachusetts Boston, a research associate with the Economic Policy Institute, and a research associate with the Political Economy Research Institute at UMass Amherst. Professor Weller has published more than 100 academic and popular articles in addition to more than 200 policy reports and short policy commentaries. He is frequently cited in the press. He has a PhD in economics from UMass Amherst.

Policy makers have tentatively expressed an interest in addressing the public's desire for more economic security in retirement. Large uncertainties about the actual economic trends as they pertain to retirees and near retirees, though, make it dif cult for analysts to identify the areas of greatest economic need among the retiree and near-retiree population. Policy makers are consequently left with insuf cient direction to respond to the public's desire for help in creating more retirement income security.

This dif culty is not surprising since the Great Recession was characterized by a number of rsts. This was the rst time that personal wealth losses exceeded 20% over the course of 2 years; this was the rst time older families had the largest increases in bankruptcy lings compared to other age groups; this was the rst time the unemployment rate of the population 65 and older exceeded 7%; this was the rst recession with a large number of new retirees relying on substantial savings in individual accounts for their retirement incomes; and this was the rst recession during which Social Security bene t cuts have been phased in. There is clearly a need for clari -cation from the research community on the impact of these unprecedented large changes in the retirement income security of retirees and near retirees.

This research has to describe the effects of the crisis on the most pertinent economic variables—income, bene ts, and savings—to provide meaningful input for policy makers. All three aspects were adversely affected during the crisis. First, older families faced, similar to other labor-market participants, rising unemployment rates. This was surprising because older workers typically started to enter retirement after a period of unemployment since they could not nd reemployment. The unemployment rates for older workers thus tended to remain low, even during a recession. Not so during the Great Recession, when the unemployment rates for older workers, those aged 55 and older, rose to their highest levels since the Great Depression. A critical policy research question is, Are policy interventions necessary and desirable to create more employment opportunities for older workers during a recession, for example, by offering more opportunities for part-time work for all workers?

Second, older workers, early retirees, and full retirees often struggle to obtain suf cient health insurance coverage. Employers have cut back on health insurance coverage for their employees and their retirees to save money, and public health insurance is often unavailable for younger retirees or it does not cover all of their needs. The clear policy research challenge is, then, rst, to identify the size of the decline in health insurance coverage for the target audience before policy makers can devise mechanisms to improve coverage.

Third, asset prices of houses and stocks tend to fall in a recession since they also re ect the economic values being created or not being created, as the case may be. It is thus not surprising that a severe recession went along with massive wealth losses. The policy research question is, Were families prepared for the eventuality of massive wealth losses? After all, public policy had shifted responsibility for retirement savings through the promotion of individual accounts and more homeownership to individuals. The expectation behind these policy decisions was that greater personal responsibility would translate into more savings in anticipation of a greater personal risk exposure.

It is crucial to consider public opinion and the potential space for speci c policy changes against the backdrop of these large-scale economic convulsions. Policy makers need to understand the public's receptiveness to sweeping changes to existing income, bene ts, and savings policies before addressing the economic fallout from the Great Recession.

This issue of the journal brings together a number of in uential researchers whose work is focused on economic policies and their impacts on retirement income security. The contributors to this special issue come from both academic and policy backgrounds. Speci cally, half of the eight contributors are academics, while the other four contributors come from think tanks in Washington, DC. The issue is thus intended to marry research and policy, both in individual contributions and in the issue's overall design.

The logic of the contributions follows roughly the discussion previously laid out. One paper discusses unemployment trends in particular. Professors Jeremy Reynolds and Jeffrey Wenger discuss the challenges to personal earnings from rising unemployment and the potential for trading off part-time work for unemployment for older workers in their discussion of unemployment trends.

Changes in wealth, in comparison, are the subject of three separate papers. David Rosnick and Dean Baker present estimates for the total loss of housing wealth for near retirees and retirees as a result of the bursting housing bubble. The decline in house prices translated into disproportionately larger home-equity losses even for older families because many families still had mortgages on their homes. The authors discuss the likely impact of the bursting housing bubble on total retirement income security. Moreover, Jack VanDerhei focuses on the trends in individual retirement savings accounts. The massive wealth losses that families sustained during the crisis resulted from price drops for both houses and stocks and thus translated into large losses on nancial assets as well as on homes. The article develops some projections for the development of individual account balances during the crisis years. Finally, I analyze whether the expectation that a greater risk exposure results in more savings is supported by the available data. This analysis compares the total expected retirement income for retirees who enjoy comparatively large income security through Social Security, pensions, and annuities with the total expected retirement income for retirees who rely more heavily on their own individual nancial and non nancial assets.

The discussion of income and wealth is rounded out by a discussion of health insurance coverage. Elise Gould and Alexander Hertel-Fernandez present evidence on health insurance coverage and estimate the likely impact of rising unemployment rates on the coverage of employer-sponsored health insurance plans.

Older families are consequently under pressure from three sides. These pressures originate in the labor market, in nancial markets, and in the health insurance market. The con uence of these trends culminates for some families in personal bankruptcy as Professor Deborah Thorne shows, although lack of adequate health insurance coverage tends to play a particularly pertinent role in determining the likelihood of bankruptcy.

The remaining two articles touch on the politics and reform options for retirement income security. David Madland presents evidence on public opinion polling, on public acceptance of large government interventions, and on the robustness of public opposition and support for speci c reform proposals. Professor Teresa Ghilarducci then follows with a sweeping pro-posal to create more retirement savings in the United States. Her article summarizes the speci cs of a large and widely debated reform proposal, addresses the potential of alternative proposals to increase savings, and contends with critiques of her policy proposal.

The issue covers a lot of ground, but considering the sizes of the prob-lems and policy challenges, it can only touch on some issues and, naturally, has to leave others out. It is my and the authors' hope that the issue provides a good sense of the challenges that near-retirees and retirees face as a result of the Great Recession and that the issue thus can help to inform potential policy responses.

Prelude to a RIF: Older Workers, Part-Time Hours, and Unemployment

JEREMY REYNOLDS, PhD

Associate Professor, Department of Sociology, University of Georgia, Athens, Georgia, USA

JEFFREY B. WENGER, PhD

Associate Professor, School of Public and International Affairs, Department of Public Administration and Policy, University of Georgia, Athens, Georgia, USA

Since the beginning of the most recent recession in December 2007, involuntary part-time employment (part-time for economic reasons) in the United States has increased from 4.2 million workers to 9.1 million, more than doubling. In this paper, we examine whether such increases in involuntary part-time employment have helped combat unemployment in the past or placed a disproportionate burden on older workers. Using Current Population Survey (outgoing rotation group) data from 1983 to 2002, we find that increases in involuntary part-time work in an industry raise the industry unemployment rate. Furthermore, the connection between rising rates of involuntary part-time work and unemployment is stronger among older workers than among younger workers. We conclude that reducing work hours through the use of part-time work does not ameliorate the effects of recessions on workers. Rather, it is a harbinger of unemployment, especially among those older than 55.

INTRODUCTION

The recent recession has brought about the largest increase in involuntary part-time employment since the Bureau of Labor Statistics started tracking it in the 1950s (Lee & Mowry, 2009). This increase was large in both absolute magnitude and as a percentage of labor force. By May of 2009, there were an estimated nine million involuntary part-time workers in the United States, nearly twice as many as in the previous year (Lee & Mowry, 2009). This increase has been disproportionately felt by workers older than 55. The share of older workers who were involuntarily part-time increased from 13.4% to 14.6% from 2006 to 2008 (Sok, 2008). What does this increase in involuntary part-time work mean? Analysts are of two minds: increases in involuntary part-time work can either be a harbinger of worse things to come or a buffer protecting workers from full-scale unemployment.

Some authors stress the negative side of involuntary part-time work by noting that it is a reliable predictor of recessions (Bednarzik, 1975, 1983; Rones, 1981; Sok, 2008). When the rate of involuntary part-time work is high, the overall economy is also less productive because labor is underutilized and spending drops. There are also many studies focusing on the negative consequences of involuntary part-time work for individual well-being. Involuntary part-time workers often have nancial troubles (Terry, 1981; Wilkins, 2007), low self-esteem (Prause & Dooley, 1997), increased risk of alcohol abuse (Dooley & Prause, 1998), and increased risk of depression (Dooley, Prause, & Ham-Rowbottom, 2000) and may not have access to employer-sponsored health insurance. Some authors consider it such a serious problem that they want to supplement the traditional, dichotomous measure of unemployment with a more continuous measure that incorporates information about involuntary part-time work (Dooley, 2003; Jensen & Slack, 2003).

Other authors, however, have highlighted the potential bene ts of invol- untary part-time work, especially the idea that it can "absorb" some of the impact of a recession. As one article put it, "The collective upside to that is that [involuntary part-time employment] slowed the deceleration of the economy by preserving some jobs" (Maidment, 2009). Indeed, the stan- dard description of the connection between involuntary part-time work and unemployment indicates that cuts in work hours are a tool that establish- ments use to prevent layoffs and the associated costs of nding, selecting, hiring, and training new workers (Rones, 1981). Speci cally, establishments are said to respond to recessions with initial cuts in hours and proceed to job cuts only if the recession is too severe to avoid layoffs (Bednarzik, 1983). The logic of these employment strategies resembles the "short-time compensation" programs that are popular in Europe and that some U.S. states introduced in the 1970s and 1980s to ght unemployment (Best & Mattesich, 1980; Schiff, 1986).

In this paper, we consider the possibility that analysts are emphasizing different sides of the same coin. We are intrigued by the notion that some industries may be especially good at combating unemployment by offering part-time hours. Nevertheless, we are also concerned that involuntary part- time work may be unevenly distributed and have different consequences for different workers, especially older workers. Indeed, if restricting employees to part-time work is a strategy organizations use to buffer the impact of a recession, they have incentives to restrict the hours of older workers, who are typically among the highest-paid. In this way, older workers may be disproportionately forced into part-time hours to protect their own jobs and perhaps the jobs of younger workers. Overall, then, increases in involuntary part-time work may not be uniformly good or bad. Rather, they may place a burden on older workers to help the industry overall. To examine these issues empirically, we focus on differences in rates of voluntary and involuntary part-time work among older workers (those 55 and older) and prime-age workers (age 25 to 54) and whether industries that increase the number of part-time workers effectively reduce their level of unemployment.

In general, we find that the rate of part-time employment for economic reasons is similar in the two age groups. We also find that higher levels of part-time employment are associated with *increases* in unemployment in the industry. Consequently, there is little support for the hypothesis that part-time employment and unemployment are substitutes at the industry level. Additionally, we find that increases in involuntary part-time work bring more economic misfortune in terms of unemployment when they occur among older workers than among prime-age workers.

These age-related differences in the effects of involuntary part-time work raise important policy concerns, especially at this time in history when demographic and lifestyle trends are increasing the number of older workers and when economic trends are making their financial situations more precarious. Between 2006 and 2016, more than 90% of the growth in the U.S. labor force will be among workers older than 55 (Toossi, 2007). Furthermore, although many older people work for intrinsic rewards (Taylor et al., 2009), a troubled social security system and retirement plans ravaged by the recession will mean that many of them will also need to work for pay. One way to support this growing segment of the labor force, which is especially likely to work part-time (Taylor et al., 2009), is to ensure that part-time workers who become unemployed are eligible to receive unemployment insurance benefits. The American Recovery and Reinvestment Act required that states extend unemployment insurance coverage to part-time workers in order to receive federal money. Twenty-three states, however, still do not offer such insurance. We think a growing number of older Americans could use that extra measure of security in these uncertain times.

PART-TIME WORK AND UNEMPLOYMENT

The Bureau of Labor Statistics (BLS) identifies two major groups of workers who are said to be part-time for *economic* reasons. First, there are workers who are part-time because their employers have cut their hours to fewer than 35 per week. They are described as part-time because of slack hours. Second, there are workers who are employed fewer than 35 hours per week because they cannot find full-time work. We will refer to workers in these two groups collectively as "involuntary part-time" workers. In contrast, the BLS classifies workers as part-time for noneconomic reasons if they normally work fewer than 35 hours per week and do not seek to work more than 35 hours. We refer to workers in this group as "regular part-time" workers.

Many analysts are interested in involuntary part-time work because of its usefulness as a *predictor* of recessions. In fact, work-hour cuts are such a consistent precursor of layoffs in durable manufacturing industries that average weekly hours in those industries are used as a leading indicator of recessions (Rones, 1981). The percentage of workers who are part-time because of slack workloads is also a good predictor of a coming recession (Bednarzik, 1983; Sok, 2008). Figure 1 shows historical trends across all industries in unemployment, involuntary part-time work, and regular part-time work. Even at this level of aggregation, there is a clear relationship between rates of unemployment and involuntary part-time work.

We are interested in involuntary part-time work for a different reason: it provides an indication of how various industries *respond* to recessions. Many authors describe increases in the use of involuntary part-time work as a strategy that establishments use to protect their workers from layoffs. The idea is that by cutting work hours when the demand for goods and services drops, employers are able to spread the available work to more employees. Theoretically, such cuts in hours also benefit organizations by helping

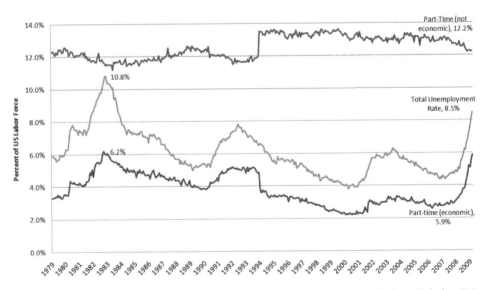

FIGURE 1 U.S. unemployment rate and part-time employment, 1979–2000. (In 1994, the CPS was redesigned and the part-time data series has a significant structural break.)

them to avoid or at least forestall layoffs and their associated costs such as paperwork, supplemental employment bene ts, contributions to state unemployment insurance, and the costs of recruiting, selecting, and training new workers (Rones, 1981).

Empirically, the use of involuntary part-time workers varies by industry. Overall, for instance, manufacturing establishments have been shifting away from employment exibility (also called numerical exibility) toward hour exibility, but a closer look reveals considerable within-industry heterogeneity (Glosser & Golden, 2005). Rones calculated the percentage change in employment and hours between business cycle peaks and troughs from 1953 to 1980 and found that the preference for hours versus employment cuts during recessions varied systematically, even among the nine major durable manufacturing industries (Rones, 1981, pp. 7–8). He also noted that before the 1980s, hours uctuations were not a very good predictor of recessions and recoveries in service, mining, construction, and non–durable goods industries (Rones, 1981: footnote 2, page 10). These industry-level differences in the use of hours reductions are probably driven by variations in capital-to-labor ratios, the use of continuous production technologies, and the dif culty of storing extra inventory (Rones, 1981). Unionization is also likely to matter. Unions often require organizations to cut work hours before resorting to layoffs, thus boosting the use of involuntary part-time work, but unions also hasten the transition to layoffs (Medoff, 1979).

We want to know whether industry differences in the use of involuntary part-time work translate into industry differences in unemployment. If organizations in some industries are better able to adjust to recessions by cutting work hours rather than jobs, they may offer workers greater job security. That is certainly the stated rationale for the rise in involuntary part-time employment during recessions, but we are unaware of any empirical tests of the relationship.[1] Furthermore, much of the previous work on the rise in involuntary part-time work has focused on the manufacturing sector, which has become a smaller share of the labor force. We are interested in whether rates of involuntary part-time work and unemployment will be negatively related in a broad set of industries.

Involuntary Part-Time Work and Age

We are also interested in whether rates of involuntary part-time work and their industry-level consequences vary with age. Previous research has shown that teenagers, African Americans, women, and less-skilled workers are especially likely to be part-time involuntarily (Bednarzik, 1975, 1983). What about older workers? Are older workers more likely than prime-age workers to be working part-time involuntarily? Do older workers in an industry serve as buffers to protect the jobs of younger workers?

These issues have not been adequately addressed in the literature, and yet they are increasingly important because of increases in the labor-force participation rates of older workers. In past decades, when it was the norm to retire at or before age 65, the imposition of part-time hours among workers older than 55 would have in uenced fewer people than it would today. The modern reality is that more people are working until later in life, often out of economic necessity. Indeed, the recent and rapid rise in part-time work for economic reasons has occurred at a time when the long-term employment rate for older workers is high and rising. During the early 1990s (1991 to 1993), the civilian employment to population ratio for those older than 55 was below 30%. Since 1993, however, the employment to population ratio has increased to 40%, making labor-force participation for those older than 55 as high today as it was in the early 1960s.

Why might older workers be especially likely to be working part-time involuntarily? Work-hour cuts among prime-age and older workers may vary in their ef cacy. Prime-age workers represent a much larger share of the labor force than older workers, so increases in involuntary part-time work among prime-age workers may be especially effective at preventing unemployment at the industry level. Still, as Bewley (1999) notes, older workers tend to be more expensive than prime-age workers, and an hour cut from the schedules of older workers is likely to save more money than an hour cut from the schedules of younger workers. Consequently, older workers may be particularly likely to have their hours cut during recessions because fewer of them would have to work reduced hours to achieve the desired level of savings.

There is also the question of who bene ts from work-hour cuts. There is some evidence that older workers may bear the brunt of work-hour reductions without really bene ting from their sacri ces, especially in union settings. Increases in involuntary part-time employment help younger union workers more than older union workers (Medoff, 1979). Younger union members favor the use of involuntary part-time work because it postpones the need for layoffs, which usually start with the youngest workers. Older union members, in contrast, are less likely to bene t from involuntary part-time work because their seniority already protects them from layoffs. Using the power that seniority brings, older union members have ensured that the transition from work-hour cuts to layoffs (of younger workers) happens relatively quickly. The cost-minimization logic that is said to drive the use of involuntary part-time work may lead to similar results in industries with low levels of unionization. If establishments want to avoid the many short-term and long-term costs of layoffs, they may be reluctant to layoff older workers, who are a dif cult-to-replace and legally protected class of workers. Consequently, the use of involuntary part-time work among older workers may be unlikely to reduce the unemployment rate among older workers, who are already relatively safe from layoffs.

DATA AND METHOD

To evaluate age-speci c rates of part-time employment and the relationship between part-time hours and unemployment across industries, we use the Current Population Survey (CPS) (outgoing rotation group) data from 1983 to 2002. We restrict our sample to the 1983 to 2002 period, since industry codes were changed from the SIC (standard industrial classi cation) to the NAICS (North American industrial classi cation system) in 2003. This provides us with a consistent set of industry measures.

The CPS is a household-based, nationally representative survey that includes information about labor force activities for each member of the household older than 16. We restrict the age of the sample in our analysis to those 25 and older. These data are used by the U.S. Department of Labor to provide monthly estimates of unemployment and have been used in numerous studies of unemployment and part-time work.

In our analysis, we pool 12 months of data in each year and use these pooled samples to calculate annual measures of part-time employment and unemployment for each of the 236 industries classi ed by the SIC codes. Pooling the les over the year ensures suf cient sample sizes in each industry to estimate employment by part-time status, age group, and gender in each year and also eliminates the issues of seasonality in the data. Industries (or rather industry years) serve as our unit of analysis.

Our dependent variable is the overall unemployment rate by industry.[2] We also include a lagged measure of industry unemployment as an independent variable so we can estimate the effect of changes in part-time employment net of the preexisting unemployment situation. Our primary explanatory variables are three measures of part-time work: (1) part-time due to slack work, (2) part-time for economic reasons (other than slack work), and (3) regular part-time. For all of the models (including those not shown but discussed later), we regress the current period unemployment on the 1-year lagged measures of part-time. Measures 1 and 2 are both measures of part-time for economic reasons, but we separate slack work (a reduction in hours prompted by the rm) from the inability to nd full-time work because slack work is much more pervasive in a recession (Bednarzik, 1983; Sok, 2008). All three measures of part-time employment are constructed as percentages of a particular age/gender group. In the analysis of older men, for instance, the percentage of regular part-timers is calculated as the number of men aged 55 or older in the industry who are regular part-time workers divided by the total number of men aged 55 or older who are employed in the industry. We also include a time trend in all our analysis to avoid attributing causal relationships to spurious correlations as well as a indicator variable to identify years when the U.S. economy was in a recession (as de ned by National Bureau of Economic Research).

Analytic Strategy

To determine the effects of part-time employment on unemployment, we estimate equation 1 using a xed-effects panel data estimator.[3] In this model, we propose that while controlling for last year's industry-wide unemployment rate, the effect of part-time due to slack work will be less than zero if the reduction in hours has a protective effect on workers. If β_2 and β_3 are greater than zero, then part-time for economic reasons merely serves as a harbinger of future unemployment.

$$Unemp_{i,t} = \alpha + \beta_1 Unemp_{i,t-1} + \beta_2 PT^{Slack}_{i,t-1} + \beta_3 PT^{Econ}_{i,t-1} + \beta_4 PT^{Regular}_{i,t-1}$$

$$+ \gamma_1 T_t + \gamma_2 Recession_t + \varepsilon_{1,t} \tag{1}$$

Part-time employment differs dramatically by gender and age. Many women work in regular part-time arrangements, and these arrangements are less sensitive to the business cycle than are involuntary part-time arrangements (Tilly, 1991). Men and women also differ in their rates of part-time work and may have different options when confronted with mandatory transitions from full-time to part-time work. For these reasons, we estimate models for men and women separately, calculating the percentage part-time based only on the female or male employment in the industry. Additionally, we estimate separate models for prime-age workers and older workers to identify age-related differences in the use and consequences of part-time work.

DESCRIPTIVE RESULTS

In Tables 1 and 2, we provide some evidence of the variation in part-time employment arrangements by industry. To keep the exposition simple, we have aggregated all the industries into nine categories covering all industries (these represent 1-digit SIC codes). In Table 1, we present results for men separately for prime-age and older workers and further separate by part-time for economic reasons and regular part-time. Table 2 presents the same results for women. In both tables, the gures represent the average percentage of part-time workers in the industry. By calculating the percentages based on the number of workers in that industry and age group, we make data in all of the cells comparable.

The rst thing to note is how little variation by age there is in the percentage of workers who are part-time for economic reasons. Among all nine industries, the biggest gap between the two age groups for men (in agriculture) is only 1.5 percentage points. This implies that on average, 6.2%

TABLE 1 Men: Industries and Part-Time (PT) Employment by Reason and Age

	% PT for economic reasons		% Regular PT	
	25–54	55+	25–54	55+
Agriculture	**6.2%**	**4.7%**	4.0%	11.9%
Mining	1.7%	2.6%	1.0%	5.3%
Construction	7.0%	6.2%	3.7%	8.7%
Manufacturing	1.6%	1.5%	1.6%	6.6%
Transportation, communication, and public utilities	2.4%	2.8%	3.4%	9.4%
Trade	3.0%	2.7%	**5.0%**	**19.0%**
Finance, insurance, and real estate	1.2%	1.7%	4.4%	18.2%
Services	3.5%	3.2%	7.2%	19.8%
Public administration	0.5%	1.0%	2.5%	11.9%

Note. Percentages calculated as the number of part-time workers aged 25 to 54 (or 55+) *divided by the total number of workers **of that age group** in that industry.* Percentages represent the 1983–2002 average. Numbers in **boldface** represent the largest gap by age.

TABLE 2 Women: Industries and Part-Time (PT) Employment by Reason and Age

	% PT for economic reasons		% Regular PT	
	25–54	55+	25–54	55+
Agriculture	**6.8%**	**4.8%**	22.1%	23.8%
Mining	1.5%	1.7%	7.3%	16.4%
Construction	3.8%	3.3%	20.5%	31.3%
Manufacturing	3.3%	3.8%	7.5%	13.8%
Transportation, communication, and public utilities	2.4%	2.5%	13.5%	22.6%
Trade	6.9%	5.3%	**27.1%**	**40.0%**
Finance, insurance, and real estate	1.7%	2.1%	14.3%	25.3%
Services	4.4%	4.3%	25.6%	35.8%
Public administration	1.2%	2.0%	10.7%	21.3%

Note. Percentages calculated as the number of part-time workers aged 25 to 54 (or 55+) *divided by the total number of workers **of that age group** in that industry.* Percentages represent the 1983–2002 average. Numbers in **boldface** represent the largest gap by age.

of prime-age men working part-time in agricultural work would prefer full-time work, whereas 4.7% of older part-time workers would prefer full-time work. For all other industries, the differences between older men and prime-age men are less than 1 percentage point.

These results are somewhat surprising given the large differences in the percentage of regular part-time employment by age. One reason we may see such small differences by age is that some employers are reluctant to hire workers they think are "overquali ed" and thus likely to leave as soon as they nd a better tting job (Bewley, 1999, pp. 335–343). Such workers must have a credible reason to want part-time work, and older workers who have worked full-time in the past and have many years of experience may have an especially dif cult time convincing employers that they want part-time work. We should note that this explanation is only meaningful for the portion of involuntary part-time workers who cannot nd full-time work (as compared to having the employer reduce their hours). Another potential reason for the small differences by age may be that these gures are average rates from 1983 through 2002. Since part-time for economic reasons is sensitive to the business cycle, averaging across multiple years may mute some of the variation in this category.

Finally, we note that older workers make up a much larger share of the regular part-time labor force. Consequently, younger workers make up a larger share of the full-time labor force. Since employers are likely to reduce the hours of their full-time labor forces during a recession (this is especially true if employers are paying overtime wage premia), the number of available workers for hours cuts is higher among the prime-age group. Not only is this due to the larger share (and number) of younger full-time workers; it is also the case because older workers are more likely to be in managerial positions and exempt from overtime pay. However, if older workers are earning more, it may make economic sense to reduce the hours of older workers.

For regular part-time workers, the smallest difference (e.g., 4.3% in mining) is much larger than the differences in part-time for economic reasons by age. The largest gap is in trade, where trade represents both wholesale and retail trade and includes speci c industries such as grocery stores that are known to employ a large percentage of part-time workers. We also see much more variation in the percentage of those working in regular part-time employment across industries. For younger workers, the percentages range from 1% in mining to 7.2% in the service sector. For older workers, the range is much larger, with mining still representing the smallest proportion of older part-time workers. At the other end of the spectrum, nearly one in ve older men in both the trade and service industries work regular part-time hours.

For women (see Table 2), the results for part-time for economic reasons are strikingly similar to those of men. Examining part-time for economic reasons, we note that the differentials between older and prime-age workers are quite small, with the largest differential being in agriculture (the same as for men). Again, we note that the overquali cation problem may reduce the willingness of employers to hire prime-age women for part-time jobs. The fact that these results are averages over the business cycle may also reduce the estimates.

For women working regular part-time jobs, the differentials by age are quite similar to those of men. This may be dif cult to see since the overall percentage of women working part-time hours is quite high. Overall, the percentage point gap in regular part-time for older and prime-age workers in these industries is 9.1% for women and 8.7% for men. Finally, we note that more than one-third of the older women employed in construction (34.6%), trade (45.3%), and services (40.1%) are working part-time (both regular and economic reasons combined). The service industry is the only one where more than one-third of prime-age workers are employed on a part-time basis.

Overall, Tables 1 and 2 show three important attributes of part-time work. First, there are considerable differences in industry concentrations of part-time work, with some industries making only limited use of part-time hours and other industries having more than one-third of their workforce employed part time (Wenger, 2001). Second, there are large gender-based differences in the total percentage of workers in an industry working part-time. In three of nine industries, more than a third of female workers work part-time. For men, the percentage of older workers employed part-time never exceeds 25%. Finally, the percentage of prime-age and older workers in each industry who work part-time for economic reasons was quite similar. It appears that even though there are higher percentages of regular part-time older men and women working in most industries (compared to younger workers), this did not translate into higher percentages of older workers being part-time for economic reasons.

In the next section, we turn our attention to the multivariate results. We use the measures of part-time employment discussed above to examine how the employment of part-time workers in the previous period affects an industry's overall unemployment rate.

MULTIVARIATE RESULTS

Our multivariate models explain about 25% of the variance in industry unemployment rates among men and about 12% of the variance among women (see Table 3). The R^2 statistics are slightly higher for prime-age workers than for older workers. Furthermore, as might be expected, our results indicate that unemployment is higher during recession years and that industry unemployment rates were trending downward between 1983 and 2002.

The results, however, do not support the prediction that the overall industry unemployment rate would be lower in industries that rely more heavily on part-time work. We anticipated that part-time employment due to slack work would be especially helpful at lowering unemployment in the industry. Consequently, we expected that the estimated effect of part-time employment would be negative, implying that increases in part-time employment resulted in lower industry-wide unemployment. Our results, in contrast, indicate that increases in this type of part-time work do not protect workers from unemployment. In fact, it seems that industries that increase involuntary part-time employment do not protect workers from future unemployment. When the rate of part-time employment due to slack work increases among prime-age men, older men, or older women, there is a subsequent *increase* in the overall industry unemployment rate (see Table 3, columns 1, 2, and 4). Among older men, increases in part-time work for other economic reasons (e.g., could not nd full-time work) and increases in regular part-time work have similar effects (see Table 3, column 2). Indeed, for older men, it seems that any increase in part-time employment is a harbinger of layoffs.

The one partial exception to this pattern is prime-age women. For this group, which has historically dominated the part-time labor market, the results often mirror those of men. Increases in rates of involuntarily part-time work, for instance, do not protect workers from future unemployment. The coef cient for part-time due to slack work does not quite reach signi - cance at the $p < .05$ level, but it is positive just as it was for the other groups (see Table 3, column 3). Furthermore, the estimated effect of part-time work for other economic reasons is both positive and signi cant, indicating that increases in that type of part-time work are followed by an increase in industry unemployment. However, the coef cient for regular part-time work indicates that increases in regular part-time work among prime-age women are followed by a *decrease* in the overall industry unemployment rate. This result suggests that when prime-age women are entering part-time work voluntarily, labor market conditions in an industry are improving.[4]

TABLE 3 Effect of Last Year's Part-Time Employment on Current Unemployment Rates Industry Fixed-Effects Estimates, by Sex and Age, 1983–2002

	Men		Women	
	25–54	55+	25–54	55+
L. Unemployment	0.320	0.347	0.188	0.201
	[0.01358]**	[0.01349]**	[0.01447]**	[0.01447]**
L. Slack work	0.249	0.327	0.056	0.290
	[0.03273]**	[0.10189]**	[0.03800]	[0.10618]**
L. Part-time employment	0.032	0.141	0.123	0.091
(economic reasons)	[0.02337]	[0.06956]*	[0.02774]**	[0.08265]
L. Regular part-time	0.015	0.046	−0.022	−0.005
	[0.01349]	[0.01546]**	[0.00827]**	[0.01675]
Linear time trend	−0.0003	−0.0004	−0.0005	−0.0006
	[0.00005]**	[0.00005]**	[0.00006]**	[0.00006]**
Recession	0.004	0.004	0.002	0.002
	[0.00063]**	[0.00064]**	[0.00081]**	[0.00081]*
Constant	0.025	0.027	0.041	0.042
	[0.00111]**	[0.00101]**	[0.00206]**	[0.00139]**
Observations	4,156	4,156	4,153	4,153
Number of 3-digit industries	241	241	241	241
R^2	0.26	0.24	0.14	0.13

Note. L. indicates that the measure is lagged one year. Standard errors in brackets.
*Signi cant at 5%; **signi cant at 1%.

These results do not simply re ect the positive association between unemployment and part-time work for economic reasons. It is certainly true that both economic indicators tend to go up during recessions and down during recoveries (Bednarzik, 1975, 1983). However, by controlling for the linear time trend in unemployment and the unemployment rate in the previous year, our regressions capture an interesting relationship. They show how changes in various types of part-time employment for a speci c age group in uence the subsequent industry unemployment rate net of the other factors that are most likely to in uence the unemployment rate. Consequently, our results cast doubt on the standard depiction of cutting hours as protecting workers from unemployment. Our results are more consistent with recent analyses that suggest that work-hour cuts often fail to lower unemployment rates because they are often not accompanied by a reduction in the weekly wage (Kapteyn, Kalwij, & Zaidi, 2004). It may also be that employers underestimate the effects of an economic downturn, adopting half measures before they ultimately must lay workers off. If that is the case, our analysis suggests that employers consistently and systematically underestimate the effects of recessions on their employment levels.

Our results also provide some evidence that changes in involuntarily part-time employment have a greater effect on overall industry unemployment levels when those changes occur among older workers than among prime-age workers. We suspected that these age differences re ect older workers' relatively strong attachment to the labor market combined with strong roots in a particular industry (see Noreau, 2000). When the labor market in an industry declines and involuntary part-time work increases, many younger workers will make a career change, go back to school, or look for employment in a different industry. Many men and women who are 55 and older, in contrast, are likely to be stuck in a dif cult place. This has been the case in Canada (Noreau, 2000). They are often not nancially prepared to retire. They may also be either too entrenched in their industry to have many employment opportunities in a different industry or believe that their industry-speci c skills are valuable enough to wait for a labor-market rebound and the return of full-time employment.[5] When the labor market does not rebound quickly and additional cuts are necessary, these older workers may become unemployed. To test these ideas formally, we compared the coef cients from different models in Table 3 and found that the joint effect of the two involuntary part-time coef cients is signi - cantly larger for older women than for younger women. Among men, the differences were not statistically signi cant.

We found further evidence of age differences in two supplementary regressions (not shown) that examined the connection between involuntary part-time work and age-speci c unemployment. One regression used the industry unemployment rate for prime-age workers as the dependent variable, and the other used the industry unemployment rate for older workers as the dependent variable. Both included age- and industry-speci c measures of part-time work as independent variables (e.g., the percentage of prime-age workers in an industry who are regular part-time) as well as the three other variables from Table 3. Because there were not enough older workers in every 3-digit industry to obtain reliable estimates of the age-speci c unemployment rate by industry and gender, we pooled men and women into the same regressions.

The results from these supplementary regressions indicate that changes in part-time employment due to slack hours among a particular age group in uence the industry unemployment rate among that same age group. For instance, increases in part-time work due to slack hours among older workers lead to increases in unemployment among older workers. We nd a similar relationship among prime-age workers. This is further evidence that increases in part-time work are not protective but rather a precursor to a reduction in force.

Furthermore, consistent with our expectation, the joint effect of the two involuntary part-time variables had a statistically smaller effect on unemployment among younger workers than among older workers. This difference is important. It indicates that even if older workers are not more likely than younger workers to be involuntarily part-time, rising levels of involuntary part-time employment have worse consequences in terms of unemployment for older workers than for younger workers.

Because previous research has highlighted sector differences in the use of work-hour reductions, we also examined differences between manufacturing and service industries. In the past, work-hour cuts have been closely related to changes in unemployment in manufacturing, but the same has not been true of service industries (Rones, 1981). To assess this possibility, we estimated four supplementary regressions (not shown) using the same age-speci c independent variables. These models examined the predictors of the industry unemployment rate for prime-age workers and for older workers in the subset of manufacturing industries and in the subset of service industries. Again, to obtain reliable estimates of the age-speci c unemployment rate by industry, we did not estimate separate models for men and women.

Our comparison of results for manufacturing and service industries indicates that there are differences between the two sectors. Part-time employment due to slack work is a precursor to unemployment in manufacturing industries among older workers and a marginally signi cant predictor of unemployment among prime-age workers. In service industries, however, this particular type of part-time work is not a predictor of unemployment. It seems that the process of adjusting to economic downturns in service industries does not typically involve the preliminary cutting of hours among full-time workers. Rather, increases in the unemployment rate among prime-age workers in service industries are preceded by increases in the percentage of prime-age workers who are part-time for other economic reasons. In other words, the harbinger of future job cuts depends on both age and sector of employment. Older workers in manufacturing industries should beware of cuts in hours. Prime-age workers in the service industry should pay attention to increases in the number of workers (perhaps from other industries) who are part-time because they cannot nd full-time work.[6]

CONCLUSION

In this paper, we focus on part-time employment at the 3-digit industry level. Using the 1983–2002 CPS data, we calculate part-time employment shares by age group and gender. We use these measures to answer two questions about the role of part-time work in an industry.

First, we wanted to know whether the rates of regular and involuntary part-time employment among older workers and prime-age workers in an industry tend to be similar. We found that rates of regular part-time employment vary widely across industries, and the percentage of workers in the two age groups who are regular part-time are often quite different. Rates of involuntary part-time employment, however, do not vary nearly as much across industries, and the rates among prime-age and older workers in an industry tend to be very similar. These ndings are encouraging. They suggest that even though older workers are now more likely to be employed than they were in the past and even though they are more likely than prime-age workers to be part-time, they are not overrepresented among involuntary part-time workers.

Second, we wondered whether increases in involuntary part-time work help reduce subsequent unemployment. This is the standard depiction of recessions: when demand drops, work hours are cut rst in the hopes that layoffs will not be necessary. We found scant evidence that involuntary part-time employment serves as a protective factor. Rather, increases in the rate of involuntary part-time employment among older workers or prime-age workers in an industry are followed by increases in the unemployment rate. Increases in part-time work only seem to be a good sign when they are increases in regular part-time work among prime-age women. This indicates that even though they may serve other purposes, involuntary part-time workers do not serve as a buffer against unemployment. In fact, we found evidence that increases in the rate of involuntary part-time work among older workers is followed by especially large increases in that group's unemployment rate. In short, while increases in involuntary part-time work are a harbinger of unemployment in general, they seem to foretell especially hard times for older workers.

These ndings offer a glimpse into the labor market dynamics of the recent past, and they are provocative because they contradict the common belief that involuntary part-time work protects jobs. What might they tell us about the likely fallout from the most recent recession? Making predictions about the future is always a tricky business, but since our analysis is based on data collected as recently as 2002, we would be surprised if the most current recession did not re ect our ndings. Still, only additional analysis will tell. Our work also raises a number of questions that will require further research and different data sets to answer. Is the use of involuntary part-time work any more effective at preventing unemployment at the establishment level? If labor markets are becoming more exible in terms of hours but less exible in terms of employment (Glosser & Golden, 2005), has that really translated into better protection for workers during recessions? The most current recession has been marked by slower than usual ows out of employment (Frazis & Ilg, 2009). Are these slower ows a re ection of increases in the use of involuntary part-time workers? What happens to older workers who are employed part-time involuntarily? Panel data from Canada indicate that older workers are less likely than younger workers to transition to full-time jobs (Noreau, 2000).

At this point, it is premature to make speci c policy recommendations regarding how establishments or industries should approach the issue of involuntary part-time employment, but some broad protective measures seem warranted. Regular part-time work is an extremely useful employment option, especially for older workers, who may want to ease into retirement. The value of involuntary part-time work, in contrast, is more ambiguous. Involuntary part-time work is not without its merits. Many workers who want full-time work would prefer to have part-time work rather than no work at all. Still, our analysis contributes to a growing list of studies indicating that involuntary part-time employment has few bene ts. Speci cally, our research indicates that it does not deliver the protection from unemployment that it is often said to provide and that industries with high rates of involuntary part-time unemployment actually have higher subsequent rates of unemployment, especially among older workers. Therefore, while we are reluctant to prescribe how establishments or industries should use part-time employment, we would like to see states extend unemployment insurance bene ts to part-time workers. Many states have been reluctant to do this, despite the fact that these workers pay unemployment insurance taxes. Such insurance, however, would provide the growing and vulnerable population of older workers with added protection from the deleterious effects of involuntary part-time work and leave them better able to cope with the unemployment that rising rates of involuntary part-time work foretell.

NOTES

[1]There are studies that examine whether work-sharing reduces unemployment (e.g., Jackman, Layard, & Nickell, 1996; Kapteyn, Kalwij, & Zaidi, 2004), but that is a different issue. Work-sharing is a long-term strategy used at the state or country level that typically alters standard or contractual hours

and thus the point at which establishments must pay overtime. The 35-hour work week in France is one such program. The use of involuntary part-time that we examine is an informal, short-term reaction to economic downturns that does not alter the regulation of overtime hours.

[2]Sample sizes in some industries were very small when we calculate industry unemployment by age and gender. In the regressions that follow, we report only those results that use overall industry unemployment rates as the dependent variable. However, we do provide evidence in the footnotes that even when we estimate age- and gender-specic unemployment rates, our results do not differ substantively from what we present here.

[3]We also estimate this model using the Arellano-Bond generalized method of moment's estimator and use additional lags of the unemployment rates as instruments to militate against endogeneity. Results from these models were substantively similar to those present in Table 3.

[4]Prompted by the helpful comments of an anonymous reviewer, we reestimated the models in Table 3 with three changes. We controlled for the standard deviation in total industry hours over the year to measure volatility in industry output. We added a measure of average hours in the industry to capture changes in work hours that did not involve switches from full-time to part-time. We also replaced our recession dummy variables with a measure of how much GDP deviated from trend. Increases in volatility were associated with greater subsequent unemployment. Reductions in average weekly hours were associated with greater subsequent unemployment, much like our measure of involuntary part-time work. Lower-than-expected GDP was associated with greater subsequent unemployment among men. The results for our three part-time variables were largely unchanged. Because this alternate specication told the same story as Table 3, we have opted to report the models in Table 3 instead.

[5]As noted by an anonymous reviewer, the tendency for unemployed workers to seek employment in a different industry may vary from one industry to the next. To the extent that these industry-level differences are time invariant, our xed effects models will control for them.

[6]The recession variable was never signicant for older workers in these regressions. However, a one-period lag of the recession was statistically significant for both older men and women. Perhaps this is because older workers are the rst to be unemployed due to their relatively higher wages. As a result, contemporaneous measures of recession may not capture the layoffs that may have already occurred for this group.

REFERENCES

Bednarzik, R. W. (1975). Involuntary part-time work: A cyclical analysis. *Monthly Labor Review, 98*, 12–18.

Bednarzik, R. W. (1983). Short workweeks during economic downturns. *Monthly Labor Review, 106*.

Best, F., & Mattesich, J. (1980). Short-time compensation systems in California and Europe. *Monthly Labor Review, 103*, 13–22.

Bewley, T. F. (1999). *Why wages don't fall during a recession.* Cambridge, MA: Harvard University Press.

Dooley, D., & J. Prause, J. (1998). Underemployment and alcohol misuse in the National Longitudinal Survey of Youth. *Journal of Studies on Alcohol, 59*, 669–680.

Dooley, D., Prause, J., & Ham-Rowbottom, K. A. (2000). Underemployment and depression: Longitudinal relationships. *Journal of Health and Social Behavior, 41*, 421–436.

Dooley, D. (2003). Unemployment, underemployment, and mental health: Conceptualizing employment status as a continuum. *American Journal of Community Psychology, 32*, 9–20.

Frazis, H. J., & Ilg, R. E. (2009). Trends in labor force ows during recent recessions. *Monthly Labor Review, 132*, 3–18.

Glosser, S., & Golden, L. (2005). Is labour becoming more or less exible? Changing dynamic behaviour and asymmetries of labour input in US manufacturing. *Cambridge Journal of Economics, 29*, 535–557.

Jackman, R., Layard, R., & Nickell, S. (1996). *Combating unemployment: Is flexibility enough?* Centre for Economic Performance, London School of Economics and Political Science.

Jensen, L., & Slack, T. (2003). Underemployment in America: Measurement and Evidence. *American Journal of Community Psychology, 32*, 21–31.

Kapteyn, A., Kalwij, A., & Zaidi, A. (2004). The myth of worksharing. *Labour Economics, 11*, 293–313.

Lee, Y., & Mowry, B. (2009). Involuntary part-time workers and the de ciencies of the unemployment rate. *Economic Trends*. Retrieved June 4, 2009 from www.clevelandfed.org/research/trends/2009/0509/03ecoact.cfm.

Maidment, P. (2009). Forced part-time employment. *Notes on the News*, Forbes.com.

Medoff, J. L. (1979). Layoffs and alternatives under trade unions in United States manufacturing. *American Economic Review, 69*, 380–395.

Noreau, N. (2000). *Longitudinal aspect of involuntary part-time employment*. Ottawa, Canada: Statistics Canada.

Prause, J., & Dooley, D. (1997). Effect of underemployment on school-leavers' self-esteem. *Journal of Adolescence, 20*, 243–260.

Rones, P. L. (1981). Response to recession: Reduce hours or jobs? *Monthly Labor Review, 104*, 3–11.

Schiff, F. W. (1986). Short-time compensation: Assessing the issues. *Monthly Labor Review, 109*, 28–30.

Sok, E. (2008). *Involuntary part-time work on the rise*. Washington, DC: U.S. Department of Labor, U.S. Bureau of Labor Statistics.

Taylor, P., Kochhar, R., Morin, R., Wang, W., Dockterman, D., & Medina, J. (2009). *Recession turns a graying office grayer*. Washington, D.C.: Pew Research Center.

Terry, S. L. (1981). Involuntary part-time work: New information from the CPS. *Monthly Labor Review, 104*, 70–74.

Tilly, C. (1991). Reasons for the continued growth of part-time employment. *Monthly Labor Review, 114*, 10–18.

Toossi, M. (2007). Labor force projections to 2016: More workers in their golden years. *Monthly Labor Review, 130*, 33–52.

Wenger, J. B. (2001). *The continuing problems with part-time work*. Economic Policy Institute Issue Brief 155. April.

Wilkins, R. (2007). The consequences of underemployment for the underemployed. *Journal of Industrial Relations, 49*, 247–275.

The Impact of the Housing Crash on the Wealth of the Baby Boom Cohorts

DAVID ROSNICK, PhD

Economist, Center for Economic and Policy Research, Washington, DC, USA

DEAN BAKER, PhD

Codirector, Center for Economic and Policy Research, Washington, DC, USA

The collapse of the housing bubble and the resulting plunge in the stock market destroyed more than $10 trillion in household wealth. The impact was especially severe for the baby boom cohorts who are at or near retirement age. This paper uses data from the Federal Reserve Board's 2007 Survey of Consumer Finances to compare the wealth of the baby boomer cohorts just before the crash with projections of household wealth following the crash. These projections show that most baby boomers will be almost entirely dependent on their Social Security income after they stop working.

INTRODUCTION

The collapse of the housing bubble and the resulting plunge in the stock market have destroyed more than $10 trillion in household wealth between the peak of the bubble in 2007 and the beginning of 2009. This loss of wealth is likely to prove especially painful for the baby boom cohorts who are nearing retirement. This paper uses projections derived from data in the 2007 Survey of Consumer Finance (SCF) to assess the wealth of these cohorts in the wake of the crash. It updates two earlier papers that constructed projections based on the 2004 SCF (Baker & Rosnick, 2008; Rosnick & Baker, 2008).

The impact of the collapse of the housing bubble on the wealth of the baby boom cohorts has very important policy implications, rst and foremost for the status of Social Security and Medicare. Both programs will face serious nancial problems during the retirement years of the baby boom cohorts, leading to substantial pressure for cuts in bene ts. The ability of the baby boomers to adjust to lower bene ts will depend on the extent to which they are able to generate income outside of Social Security.

This study also has important policy implications for pension policy more generally. If most baby boomers were unable to accumulate suf cient savings to support a decent retirement under the current system, then it suggests a need for improvements in the retirement system. Ideally, private savings plus pensions will be suf cient to allow most workers to maintain their standard of living in retirement.

The rst part of this paper brie y reviews some of the prior research on the wealth of the baby boomers. The second section explains the methodology used to analyze the wealth of the baby boomers in 2007 and makes projections for 2009. The third section presents the analysis and projections. The fourth section is a brief conclusion.

THE WEALTH OF THE BABY BOOM COHORTS: PRIOR WORK

There is extensive literature on the long-term trends in preparedness for retirement. Edward Wolff (2002) concluded that based on analysis of the SCF, most families were poorly prepared for retirement even prior to the crash of the technology bubble at the end of the decade. This study showed that the growth in wealth in the 1980s and 1990s was concentrated at the top. Of course, much of this wealth was lost in the crash of the stock bubble at the turn of the millennium. The crash may have somewhat mitigated the growth in inequality but did not leave middle- and lower-income families better prepared for retirement.

An update of this study (Weller & Wolff, 2005) points to the growing share of Social Security in retirement income, which is largely attributable to the decline of private de ned bene t pension plans. Weller and Wolff report that from 1983 to 2001, the median net worth (including de ned bene t pensions and Social Security) of those aged 47 to 55 rose only 13.4% in a period in which per capita income rose by 51.0%. The study projected that one in ve homeowners and three in ve renters aged 47 to 64 would have insuf cient wealth to provide an income of more than double the poverty line—even with Social Security bene ts included.

Munnell and Soto (2008) examine the effect of the housing boom on homeowners' balance sheets, although they focus on the issue of equity extraction. They conclude that in 2004 mid-distribution households headed by those aged 50 to 64 consumed an additional $15,000 on account of bubble wealth effects. Munnell, Golub-Sass, Soto, and Webb (2008) nd that baby boomers are likely to have insuf cient savings to maintain their standard of living in retirement.

Engen, Gale, and Uccello (1999) present a somewhat more optimistic picture. Applying a life cycle consumption model to data from the SCF and the Health and Retirement Survey, the study nds that most families should be able to maintain a consumption level in retirement comparable to that which they enjoyed in their working years.

This paper goes beyond these prior studies in examining the impact of the collapse of the housing bubble and the subsequent fall in the stock market on the wealth of the baby boom cohorts. These events have substantially reduced their wealth.

METHODOLOGY FOR ANALYZING THE WEALTH
OF THE BABY BOOMERS

The analysis is based on the Federal Reserve Board's (FRB) 2007 SCF. The de nition of wealth and weighting of the SCF public data are identical to those used by the FRB in its published summary tables. They are based directly on a Stata translation of the FRB's SAS program for producing the 2007 SCF Chartbook.[1] The one difference is that we de ne quintiles of net worth by thresholds and not by survey weights.[2] Some, notably Edward Wolff, suggest changes to the survey weights to enforce consistency between the FRB income data and the Internal Revenue Service. Wolff also makes additional adjustments to the survey data to match in the aggregate the FRB Flow of Funds data. These adjustments are useful, especially in the context of measuring wealth and inequality, but they are likely to have little impact on a comparative analysis of wealth for households below the top quintile. Therefore, we have not attempted to make these adjustments in this analysis.

Table 1 shows the key assumptions used in projecting wealth forward from September 2007 to September 2009. The projections use three scenarios that are intended to encompass the range of plausible values for housing and stock prices. Scenario 1 is designed to be relatively optimistic. It assumes that nominal house prices do not fall from their March 2009 level. At that point, house prices were falling at a nominal rate of almost 2% per month. It assumes that S&P 500 is at a level of 1100, which would mark a substantial jump from its trough early in 2009. Scenario 2 assumes that nominal house prices decline an additional 9.7% from their March 2009 level to September. It assumes that the S&P is at 1000. Scenario 3 is designed as a pessimistic scenario. It assumes that house prices fall 14.1% from their March 2009 level and that the S&P 500 is at 850.

In all three scenarios, it is assumed that households save out of disposable income at the average personal saving rate for 2008. All three

TABLE 1 Assumptions Used in Asset Projections, 2007–2009

	CPI-U-RS	Case-Shiller 20-City Index	S&P 500
September 2007	306.2	195.69	1,473.96
Latest[a]	313.2 (+2.3%)	139.99 (−28.5%)	872.74 (−40.8%)
September 2009			
- Scenario 1	314.6 (+2.8%)	139.99 (−28.5%)	1,100 (−25.4%)
- Scenario 2	314.6 (+2.8%)	127.85 (−34.7%)	1,000 (−32.2%)
- Scenario 3	314.6 (+2.8%)	120.26 (−38.5%)	850 (−42.3%)

Note. [a]Table derived from Case-Shiller as of March, CPI-U-RS as of April, and S&P 500 (open of month) as of May 2009.

projections also assume that interest-bearing assets earned the average yield on 10-year treasury bonds for 2008. Holdings in retirement accounts were assumed to be divided proportionately between stocks, which are assumed to track the S&P 500, and interest-bearing assets.

The tables do not give a full accounting of retirement wealth because they exclude de ned-bene t (DB) pensions. This exclusion will matter less for the baby boomer cohorts than it did in prior years; however, a substantial portion of these families still stand to receive at least some payments from DB pensions. Among the 55 to 64 age group, 42.4% will get at least some money from a DB pension. In the middle quintile of this age group, 48.0% of families will receive some income from a DB pension. Among families in the 45 to 54 age group, 34.7% will receive some income from a DB pension. For families in the middle wealth quintile, this gure is 40.0%.

It is unlikely that the inclusion of wealth in DB plans would substantially change this analysis. At the end of 2008, private-sector DB plans had cumulative assets of $1,930.5 billion, covering 44 million workers and retirees. This is an average of just under $44,000 per worker.[3] The holdings are heavily skewed and disproportionately go to older workers and retirees. As a result, the net acquisition of nancial assets by these funds has been strongly negative for more than a decade. In 2008, net acquisition of assets was −$91.4 billion, nearly 5% of the assets held in DB accounts.[4] Given the sharp rate of decline in private DB pensions, most of the workers in these age groups who have DB plans are not likely to see substantial bene ts from them, certainly far less than the $44,000 average holdings. It is worth noting that those with public-sector plans are likely to fare somewhat better.

FINDINGS

Tables 2 and 3 show the median and mean incomes and net worth of people aged 45 to 54 and people aged 55 to 64, respectively, in each of the seven SCFs. The tables also show home equity and the value of holdings in

TABLE 2 Family Finances (in Thousands of 2009 Dollars) Age 45 to 54 in Year

Year	Income		Net worth		Home equity		Retirement accounts	
	Median	Mean	Median	Mean	Median	Mean	Median	Mean
1989	63.8	102.2	161.5	452.5	71.1	129.1	1.7	47.5
1992	64.0	87.1	126.5	413.7	55.0	97.2	2.7	56.0
1995	56.9	93.9	137.9	420.9	55.6	88.4	7.8	73.4
1998	67.7	92.3	143.1	474.0	54.9	91.0	13.2	70.6
2001	67.9	120.0	168.8	607.0	60.1	118.2	10.2	101.1
2004	70.7	109.7	169.9	626.3	68.8	144.9	25.7	94.5
2007	68.7	121.0	215.1	712.2	88.4	173.4	18.0	110.1

Note. Source: FRB 1989–2007 SCF and author's calculations.

TABLE 3 Family Finances (in Thousands of 2009 Dollars) Age 55 to 64 in Year

Year	Income		Net worth		Home equity		Retirement accounts	
	Median	Mean	Median	Mean	Median	Mean	Median	Mean
1989	46.6	82.0	163.0	523.9	82.7	131.1	0.0	51.7
1992	48.8	78.6	189.1	546.4	74.3	120.6	7.6	61.4
1995	49.8	80.2	180.4	563.7	76.4	115.9	4.2	68.7
1998	53.1	98.2	193.7	725.7	78.5	126.2	9.2	115.9
2001	55.7	113.5	234.8	937.9	91.1	159.1	9.6	150.7
2004	67.2	117.2	310.7	978.6	118.5	225.4	27.1	158.0
2007	59.2	118.3	267.9	991.3	107.9	195.9	23.6	173.5

Note. Source: FRB 1989–2007 SCF and author's calculations.

de ned contribution retirement accounts. The trend in net worth for these age groups is quite different over this period. In 1989, the SCF data indicate that the median family of those between the ages of 45 and 54 had a net worth of $161,500, only 0.9% less than the $163,000 net worth of families of people between the ages of 55 and 64. However, the net worth of the younger age group fell in subsequent surveys, only recovering the 1989 level in 2001. The net worth of the older age group rose in each survey, peaking at $310,700 in 2004. Differing patterns in home equity can explain part of the difference, although a fuller explanation would require a more complete examination of the changing composition of wealth and also family structures during this period.

In 2007, the median net worth for the younger age group jumped by 26.6% from its 2004 level to $215,100, as shown in Table 3. By contrast, the median net worth for families of people between the ages of 55 and 64 fell by 13.8% from its 2004 level to $267,900. The reason for the divergence is a sharp reported decline in home equity for the older age group, while the younger age group had substantially more home equity in 2007 than 2004. Again, the reasons for these changes are beyond the scope of this analysis, but it is important to remember that the data in the tables are showing us different families at the same age, not tracking the same families through time.

Before examining the projections in the three scenarios for 2009, it is worth brie y commenting on the SCF data for 2007. These calculations show the net worth for families very close to or past retirement, and the vast majority of them can anticipate no signi cant income from a DB pension. In 2007, according to the National Association of Realtors' existing homes sales data, the median house price was $217,000. This means that the net worth of families of people between the ages of 45 and 54 in that year would have been approximately suf cient to pay off the mortgage on the median house with nothing left over. The median net worth of families of those between the ages of 55 and 64 would have been suf cient to pay off this mortgage, with approximately $50,000 left over.

Table 4 shows the mean and median net worth, along with quintile averages for 2007, and each of the three scenarios projected for 2009, for families of people between the ages of 45 and 54 in 2009. Table 5 shows the same information for families of people between the ages of 55 and 64. There are sharp declines in all three scenarios for families in both age groups, although the projected declines in net worth are much sharper over this 2-year period for the younger age cohort.

In scenario 2, the median family of people between the ages of 45 and 54 is projected to have net worth of $88,000 in 2009, a drop of 59.1% from the median net worth of families in this age group in 2007. In the

TABLE 4 Net Worth: Median, Mean, and by 2007 Quintile of Net Worth (Ages 45 to 54)

Year	Median	Mean	Bottom	Second	Middle	Fourth	Top
2007	$215.1	$712.2	$6.3	$77.6	$210.7	$445.1	$2,823.9
Scenario 1	101.8	473.9	−0.8	26.4	107.3	266.1	1,972.6
Scenario 2	88.0	444.9	−1.6	19.7	93.4	240.9	1,874.2
Scenario 3	81.3	419.4	−2.1	15.0	83.4	221.4	1,781.5

Note. Source: FRB 2007 SCF and author's calculations.

TABLE 5 Net Worth: Median, Mean, and by 2007 Quintile of Net Worth (Ages 55 to 64)

Year	Median	Mean	Bottom	Second	Middle	Fourth	Top
2007	$267.9	$991.3	$6.7	$111.8	$278.5	$591.7	$3,985.2
Scenario 1	190.3	779.0	3.3	65.3	202.0	429.7	3,200.5
Scenario 2	168.7	737.2	1.1	55.0	185.7	397.0	3,052.7
Scenario 3	157.9	697.9	−0.5	47.9	173.1	370.1	2,904.1

Note. Source: FRB 2007 SCF and author's calculations.

more optimistic scenario 1, the median net worth is $101,800, while it is just $81,300 in the pessimistic scenario 3. In scenario 2, the average net worth projected for families in the bottom quintile in 2009 is negative. For families in the second wealth quintile, net worth is projected to be $19,700. In scenario 2, families in the fourth wealth quintile are projected to, on average, have net worth of $240,900 in 2009, approximately 10% above the median for this age group in 2007.

Table 5 shows that in scenario 2, the median family of people between the ages of 55 and 64 is projected to have $168,700 in net worth in 2009. Even in the more optimistic scenario 1, they are projected to have just $190,300 in net worth, a drop of 29.0% from the median net worth of families in this age group in 2007. In scenario 2, the average net worth projected for families in the second wealth quintile in the 55 to 64 age group is $55,000. For families in the fourth quintile the projected net worth in the scenario 2 is $397,000.

The most obvious explanation for the greater projected decline in net worth for the younger age group between 2007 and 2009 is a sharper projected decline in home equity. Table 6 compares the median and mean holdings in quasi-liquid retirement accounts and home equity in 2007 and the projections for 2009 for families of those between the ages of 45 and 54. Table 7 gives the same information for families of people between the ages of 55 and 64. As can be seen, families in the younger age grouping saw a very sharp decline in both median and mean home equity over this 2-year period. Median home equity is projected to fall in this scenario from $88,400 to $14,800, while mean home equity is projected to fall from $173,400 to

TABLE 6 Balances of "Quasi-Liquid" Retirement Accounts and Home Equity (Ages 45 to 54; in Thousands of 2009 Dollars)

	Retirement accounts		Home equity		
Year	Median	Mean	Median	Mean	<6% of home price
2007	$25.7	$110.1	$88.4	$173.4	2.4%
2009 scenario 1	18.0	82.0	14.8	74.5	16.9

Note. Source: FRB 2007 SCF and author's calculations.

TABLE 7 Balances of "Quasi-Liquid" Retirement Accounts and Home Equity (Ages 55 to 64; in Thousands of 2009 Dollars)

	Retirement accounts		Home equity		
Year	Median	Mean	Median	Mean	<6% of home price
2007	$23.6	$173.5	$107.9	$195.9	1.4%
2009 scenario 1	29.8	149.4	50.4	111.2	13.6

Note. Source: FRB 2007 SCF and author's calculations.

$74,500, drops of 83.3% and 67.0%, respectively. The projected decline in the median holding in retirement accounts, from $25,700 to $18,000, is both smaller in percentage terms and far smaller absolutely.

By contrast, the median home equity for families in the 55 to 64 age group is projected to fall from $107,900 to $50,400, a drop of 53.3%. Mean home equity is projected to fall from $195,900 to $111,200, a drop of 43.2%. The steeper decline in home equity among the younger age group can be readily explained by greater leverage. Younger households would typically be less far along in paying off mortgages. This means that they are much more heavily leveraged in their homes. As a result, the same percentage increase or decrease in the house price will typically lead to a much larger change in equity for a younger family than an older family. During the years of the run-up in the housing bubble, the greater leverage allowed younger families to accrue equity at a faster pace. However, when house prices began to fall in 2006, the decline had a proportionately greater impact on the equity of younger families than older families.

The plunge in house prices in the last 3 years is leading to an extraordinary situation in which a very high percentage of near-retirement cohorts will lack any equity in their homes. In addition to the large number of homeowners who are underwater, there are also a substantial number of homeowners who have some equity, but not enough to cover the normal costs associated with selling their homes. This means that if they were to sell their homes to move into a smaller house or rental unit, they would have no money from their homes to help with this move and in fact would actually have to put up some amount of money at the closing to pay off the mortgage, realtors' fees, and other costs associated with selling their homes.

Tables 8 and 9 show, for the 45 to 54 age cohort and the 55 to 64 age cohort, respectively, the share of homeowners in each wealth quintile who had less than 6% equity in their homes in each of the SCF surveys since 1989. It also shows the projected share for 2009 in scenario 2. These are, in effect, the homeowners who will have to pay money to sell their homes.

TABLE 8 Homeowners with <6% Equity in their Homes (Ages 45 to 54)

Year	All	Bottom	Second	Middle	Fourth	Top
1989	0.6%	0.0%	0.0%	0.0%	0.9%	1.2%
1992	2.4	16.5	5.3	0.0	0.6	0.3
1995	3.6	25.8	5.6	2.1	1.6	0.9
1998	4.7	35.8	6.3	6.2	0.9	1.1
2001	3.7	27.5	7.9	1.1	1.2	1.5
2004	3.3	27.1	6.8	1.9	0.1	0.5
2007	3.1	23.5	5.8	1.0	1.5	1.0
Scenario 2	32.4	90.2	56.9	37.1	22.0	13.2

Note. Source: FRB 2007 SCF and author's calculations.

TABLE 9 Homeowners with <6% Equity in their Homes (Ages 55 to 64)

Year	All	Bottom	Second	Middle	Fourth	Top
1989	0.5%	0.5%	2.3%	0.0%	0.9%	0.1%
1992	0.1	1.3	0.0	0.0	0.0	0.0
1995	1.5	8.3	3.5	0.0	0.0	0.2
1998	2.0	22.6	2.4	0.0	0.0	1.1
2001	1.1	11.5	1.0	0.0	0.0	0.0
2004	1.4	15.8	2.5	0.0	0.0	0.1
2007	1.7	13.0	1.8	0.3	1.3	0.6
Scenario 2	19.5	64.0	29.9	15.3	14.0	7.1

Note. Source: FRB 2007 SCF and author's calculations.

The assumption of 6% sales cost is almost certainly on the low side, since this is the standard realtors' fee. There are often other costs associated with selling a home, and many state and local governments impose transfer fees that are usually split between buyers and sellers.

As can be seen, historically very few homeowners in this age group fell into this category. This is due to three factors:

1. In prior decades, homeowners typically had to pay a substantial down payment when they bought their homes, so they would generally start their period of homeownership with more than 6% equity in their home.
2. By the time homeowners reached these age groupings, they would have typically been in their homes for some period of time and therefore would have paid down much of the principle on their mortgages.
3. The price of homes typically rose, roughly in step with in ation.

However, the current group of near retirees is in a very different situation. Many of them bought homes with little or no money down. In many cases they were encouraged to move during the housing boom earlier in the decade, so they have not had years of paying down the principle on mortgages, even if they may have been homeowners for decades. In addition, many families who had accumulated equity borrowed against it during the peak years of the housing bubble. Finally, the sharp plunge in house prices eliminated much of the equity that these families had accumulated during the boom years.

As a result, 32.4% of the homeowners between the ages of 45 and 54 will have to bring cash to their closing based on their projected equity in scenario 2. In the older age group, 19.5% will be forced to bring cash to their closing. By comparison, fewer than 4.0% of homeowners in the younger age grouping would have needed to bring cash to a closing based on the prior SCF surveys, except in 1998, when 4.7% would have needed to bring cash to a closing. For the older age group, 1998 was also the previous peak year, with 2.0% of homeowners between the ages of 55 and 64 having to bring cash to their closing.

While the lower wealth quintiles will disproportionately be in the situation of needing money to sell their homes, in scenario 2, 56. 9% of homeowners in the middle wealth quintile will have to bring cash to a closing. Even among families in the fourth wealth quintile, 22.0% will have to bring cash to a closing. For the older age grouping, 15.3% of homeowners in the middle wealth quintile and 14.0% of homeowners in the fourth wealth quintile will have to bring cash to a closing.

DISCUSSION

The projections for 2009 in this study suggest that the baby boom cohorts will be very poorly prepared for retirement. While there have been grounds for some time for concerns about the adequacy of their retirement savings, the prospects have become much more dire following the collapse of the housing bubble and the resulting plunge in the stock market.

While there is some prospect that both markets will recover some of their lost ground, it is certainly not reasonable to assume that there will be anything resembling a complete recovery in the years before the heads of these families reach retirement age. Certainly, the markets are not anticipating a full recovery or this would already be re ected in asset prices. While some of these families have already retired or are at the edge of retirement, the younger age groups in this analysis will still have a substantial period of time remaining in the labor force. This can allow them to raise their savings considerably beyond the levels shown in these projections.

However, the recent economic projections show the economy remaining below its capacity until 2014. The implied weakness in the labor market will make it more dif cult for workers to nd well-paying jobs and, possibly, to nd work at all. As a result, many baby boomers will nd it unusually dif cult to build up their savings over the next few years. Given the limited time that they have left in the labor force, the projected weakness in the labor market over the next 4 years could have a substantial impact on their retirement security.

With the vast majority of families in these age groups expecting little or no money from traditional DB pensions and having accumulated little money in de ned contribution accounts, families in these age groups are likely to be hugely dependent on Social Security as a source of retirement income. Policy makers will have to take this into account when considering proposals to restructure the program. For a least a decade into the future, new retirees are likely to be more dependent on Social Security than otherwise would have been expected because of the distortions created by the housing bubble.

Finally, the loss of wealth due to the plunge in house prices has created an extraordinary situation for the homeowners among these age groups. In a very high percentage of cases, instead of being assets, their homes are likely to prove to be nancial albatrosses. If they decide to move into homes that may be more appropriate for their retirement, they will nd that they will have to draw down wealth from other assets to cover the costs. The lack of home equity is likely to make these age cohorts less mobile in retirement than ordinarily would be expected from families in these age groups.

CONCLUSION

This study presented a set of wealth projections for the baby boom cohorts based on the 2007 SCF and subsequent movements in stock and housing prices. The projections show that the baby boomers' wealth fell sharply as a result of the bursting of the housing bubble and the subsequent plunge in house prices. As a result, the baby boom cohorts are much less well-prepared for retirement than the cohorts that preceded them. Most of the families in these age groups are likely to be heavily dependent on Social Security in their retirement.

NOTES

1. See http://www.federalreserve.gov/pubs/oss/oss2/bulletin.macro.txt.

2. For example, the FRB draws the line between the bottom and second quintiles of net worth by sorting all observations (including repetitions) by net worth and including in the second quintile the rst observation that would, if included in the bottom quintile, result in a total survey weight of at least 20%. Thus, observations with identical levels of net worth may be placed in different quintiles. We de ne quintiles of net worth as per Stata, where the all observations of a given net worth are added as blocks to the bottom quintile until the total survey weight is at least 20%. Thus, observations with identical levels of net worth will be in the same quintiles of net worth, but the total weight in each quintile may be unequal.

3. Data on the assets of private de ned bene t plans come from the FRB's Flow of Funds, Table L.188b., Line 1, available at http://www.federalreserve.gov/releases/z1/Current/z1r-6.pdf. The number of people enrolled in these plans is taken from the Pension Bene t Guarantee Corporation's Web site at http://www.pbgc.gov/.

4. Flow of Funds Table F.118.b, Line 1.

REFERENCES

Baker, D., & Rosnick, D. (2008). *The housing crash and the retirement prospects of late baby boomers*. Washington, DC: Center for Economic and Policy Research.

Engen, E., Gale, W. & Uccello, C. (1999). The adequacy of retirement savings. *Brookings Papers on Economic Activity, 30*, 65–188.

Federal Reserve Board. (2007). *2007 Survey of Consumer Finances: Definitions of variables given by SAS program.* Federal Reserve Board. Retrieved from http://www.federalreserve.gov/pubs/oss/oss2/bulletin.macro.txt.

Munnell, A. H., Golub-Sass, F., Soto, M., & Webb, A. (2008). *Do households have a good sense of their retirement preparedness?* Issue in Brief, 8–11. Chestnut Hill, MA: Center for Retirement Research at Boston College.

Munnell, A. H., & Soto, M. (2008). *The housing bubble and retirement security.* Working Paper, 2008–2013. Chestnut Hill, MA: Center for Retirement Research at Boston College.

Rosnick, D., & Baker, D. (2009). *The wealth of the baby boom cohorts after the collapse of the housing bubble.* Washington, DC: Center for Economic and Policy Research.

Weller, C., & Wolff, E. N. (2005). *Retirement income: The crucial role of social security.* Washington, DC: Economic Policy Institute.

Wolff, E. N. (2002). *Retirement insecurity: The income shortfalls awaiting the soon-to-retire.* Washington, DC: Economic Policy Institute.

What Will Happen to Retirement Income for 401(k) Participants After the Market Decline?

JACK VANDERHEI, PhD

Research Director, Employee Benefit Research Institute, Washington, DC, USA

This paper uses administrative data from millions of 401(k) partic-ipants dating back to 1996 as well as several simulation models to determine 401(k) plans' susceptibility to several alleged limitations as well as its potential for significant retirement wealth accumu-lation for employees working for employers who have chosen to sponsor these plans. What will happen to 401(k) participants after the 2008 market decline will be largely determined by the extent to which the features of automatic enrollment, automatic escalation of contributions, and automatic investment are allowed to play out. Simulation results suggest that the first two features will signif-icantly improve retirement wealth for the lowest-income quartiles going forward, and the third feature (primarily target-date funds) suggest that a large percentage of those on the verge of retirement would benefit significantly by a reduction of equity concentrations to a more age-appropriate level.

INTRODUCTION

There has been considerable discussion recently regarding what the current market downturn might do to retirement income. Research has shown that a worker's age is a major factor in his or her ability to recover from an economic downturn. Holden and VanDerhei (2002) simulated the likely impact of a major bear market—de ned as three consecutive years of a –9.3% annual return—on the overall (nominal) replacement rates that could be provided by "401(k) accumulations" as a function of when the downturn occurred during the employee's tenure with the retirement plan sponsor. That analysis found that age and tenure had a big effect on how badly an economic downturn affected a 401(k) participant's assets. Based on a median (or midpoint) income replacement rate of about 51% of an individual's nal income, the modeled 3-year downturn would result in a lower replacement rate for 401(k) participants in the lowest-income quartile of –3.2 percentage points at the beginning of their careers, or –7.5 percentage points for those in mid-career (ages 39–41), or –13.4% for those at the end of their careers.[1]

However, building and/or modifying a simulation model that is able to quantify the likely impact of a market downturn on eventual retirement income is a complex and dif cult process. Consequently, attention is typically focused on how a decline in the nancial markets has affected the *average defined contribution plan balances.*

The rst section of this paper takes the most recent information in the EBRI/ICI 401(k) database (year-end 2007)[2] and provides time series information (since 1996) on average and median account balances for both the *entire* sample of 401(k) participants in the database and the *consistent* sample of participants in the database from 1999 to 2007.[3] A time series of asset allocation information for millions of 401(k) participants is also explored to ascertain the validity of three common perceptions with respect to participant-directed investments in 401(k) plans. The second section of the paper uses employee-speci c information as well as nancial market indexes[4] to estimate the percentage change in average account balances among 21.8 million 401(k) participants, presented by account balances as well as age and tenure for the periods January 1, 2008, through June 30, 2009.

There has also been considerable discussion about what the current market downturn might do to retirement ages. This is a natural question to ask after observing the account balance declines for many 401(k) participants (especially those considered to be on the verge of retirement); however, for many individuals/households, this will depend on far more than just 401(k) balances with current employers. Still, the question of how long it will take 401(k) participants to recover their losses in the current market has been the topic of much speculation, and the next section of the paper provides detailed distributional analysis of the "recovery time" for participants under a variety of future return assumptions for both equity and nonequity components of the 401(k) portfolio.

Finally, the future prospects for retirement income from 401(k) plans are considered by looking at two of the plan design provisions likely to create the largest modi cations. The rst of these concerns the increasing use of target-date funds as a result of a default investment option chosen by the sponsor (most likely as a result of the quali ed default investment alternative (QDIA), regulations issued in response to the Pension Protection Act [PPA] of 2006). The second looks at the likely impact of automatic enrollment for 401(k) plans regardless of whether it is accompanied by automatic escalation of employee contributions.[5]

BACKGROUND

Account Balances

ACCOUNT BALANCES FOR THE ENTIRE EBRI/ICI 401(K) DATABASE

Using data from the EBRI/ICI 401(k) database, the average account balance for 401(k) participants has been calculated for a signi cant percentage of the 401(k) universe on an annual basis since 1996. The number of data providers (and therefore the number of 401(k) plans and participants in the database) has increased signi cantly during this time, and the database has continued to be a representative sample of the entire universe, especially as compared with subsequent Form 5500 tabulations (VanDerhei, Galer, Quick, & Rea, 1999).

The average 401(k) balance was $37,323 at year-end 1996 and increased each year until 1999, when it reached a level of $55,502. The bear market of the rst part of this decade resulted in three consecutive decreases, reaching a low of $39,855 in 2002. The average balance rebounded signi cantly in 2003 ($51,569) and increased each year though the end of 2007 ($65,454).

However, the distribution of 401(k) balances is very much skewed to the right, and many analysts are also interested in the time series of the median values. These values started at $11,600 in 1996 and increased to $15,246 in 1999 before falling to $12,578 in 2002. The median value peaked at $19,926 in 2004 and gradually fell to $18,942 in 2007.[6]

It is extremely important to realize that the means and medians mask a great deal of dispersion with respect to the distribution of these values, and looking only at a simple statistical summary of the distribution in any year will not provide an adequate assessment of how much retirement income might be provided by these plans.

Instead, VanDerhei, Holden, Alonso, and Copeland (2008) provide the year-end 2007 account balances broken out by age and tenure. The averages vary from less than $5,000 for the participants in their 20s with the lowest tenure to more than $210,000 for participants in their 60s with the longest tenure. The reason it is important to consider tenure (with the current employer) as well as age is that 401(k) balances from previous employment are often left with the previous employer's plan or rolled over to an individual retirement account (IRA).[7] For example, the overall average account balance for all current 401(k) participants in their 60s was $117,000 at year-end 2007. However, that average includes the relatively low balances of employees who have recently changed jobs.

VanDerhei et al. (2008) show average 401(k) balances as a percentage of current salary at year-end 2007 for a subset of the EBRI/ICI universe.[8] These values range from a rather de minimis value (12%) for the participants in their 20s with the lowest tenure to 296% for participants in their 60s with the longest tenure.

Some analysts have used the types of gures mentioned above as an indictment against the potential for the 401(k) system to provide meaningful levels of retirement income (when combined with assumed Social Security bene ts). However, there are two very important considerations that must be addressed:

- Average 401(k) account balances with current employers will be a function of job turnover. Even in times of a positive investment return, average balances could fall if enough employees who were participating in 401(k) plans with their former employers changed jobs and did not roll the balance over to the new employers.[9]
- Even employees on the verge of retirement who have been with a single employer for their entire careers may not have had the opportunity to participate in the 401(k) system the entire time. The Internal Revenue Code was expanded to include 401(k) in 1978, but the proposed regulations were not released until November 1981, and it took several years for many plan sponsors to modify existing pro t-sharing plans and/or adopt new 401(k) plans.[10]

The rst point was dealt with by the introduction of a "consistent sample" analysis of the EBRI/ICI database by Holden and VanDerhei (2001) and is discussed below. The second point required the creation of a stochastic simulation model to adequately project the potential of a full career of working for an employer who sponsored a 401(k) plan (regardless of whether the employee chose to participate each year). Holden and VanDerhei (2002) provided the results of the initial model, and Holden and VanDerhei (2005) expanded it to analyze the potential impact of 401(k) plan sponsors modifying their plans to utilize automatic enrollment (AE). Later, VanDerhei (2007) modi ed the model to account for the automatic escalation of contributions that were provided under the safe harbor provisions of the PPA, and VanDerhei and Copeland (2008) presented the results of a new simulation program that projected the eventual 401(k) balances of all

U.S. employees.[11] The last section of this article summarizes the simulation research.

ACCOUNT BALANCES FOR THE CONSISTENT SAMPLE OF 401(K) PARTICIPANTS IN THE EBRI/ICI 401(K) DATABASE FROM 1999 TO 2007

Table 1 shows the average and median 401(k) account balances for a group of 2.4 million participants with account balances at the end of each year from 1999 through 2007. The average gures start out 20% higher than the equivalent numbers for the full EBRI/ICI 401(k) database at year-end 1999 but increase to 110% larger by year-end 2007. Due to a modi ed form of survivorship bias, these numbers should not be used as an indication of what the average balance ($137,430) or median balance ($76,946) of the entire population of 401(k) participants would be as of year-end 2007. However, the rst order differences in the annual time series can be compared to give a better indication of the impact of each year's investment income and cash ows (primarily contributions) on 401(k) account balances without the downward bias caused by job turnover that a simple comparison of annual averages or medians would provide.

Asset Allocation

The concept of participant-directed investments (for at least the employee contributions and, in many cases, the employer contributions as well) has been the subject of considerable analysis in the past for several reasons:

TABLE 1 401(k) Account Balances[a] Among 401(k) Participants Present From Year-End 1999 Through Year-End 2007[b]

	Average	Median
1999	$66,660	$24,844
2000	$66,677	$28,106
2001	$65,936	$30,737
2002	$61,341	$30,727
2003	$80,592	$43,127
2004	$93,841	$51,927
2005	$103,751	$58,071
2006	$122,037	$68,866
2007	$137,430	$76,946

Note. Source: Tabulations from EBRI/ICI Participant-Directed Retirement Plan Data Collection Project.
[a]Account balances are participant account balances held in 401(k) plans at the participants' current employers and are net of plan loans. Retirement savings held in plans at previous employers or rolled over into IRAs are not included.
[b]The analysis is based on a sample of 2.4 million participants with account balances at the end of each year from 1999 through 2007.

- The possibility that some participants will be extremely risk-averse and choose not to invest in equities, even while they are relatively young.
- The possibility that some participants (especially those who are not also covered by de ned bene t plans) will invest too aggressively in equities as they approach retirement age.
- The concept of diversi cation will be violated to the detriment of the participant (especially with respect to company stock).

IS THERE INSUFFICIENT EQUITY ALLOCATION AMONG YOUNG 401(K) PARTICIPANTS?

VanDerhei et al. (2008) show the 401(k) plan average asset allocation in selected years as a percentage of total assets. Even though values have uctuated signi cantly during this time (largely due to market volatility), it is clear that, overall, the 401(k) plan assets have been concentrated in equity funds. Assuming that 60% of the balanced funds are invested in equities, the overall total equity component for the years shown varies from a low of 61% (2002) to a high of 76% (1999).

Although this suggests in aggregate that the equity component of 401(k) investments will be suf ciently large (especially when compared with the conventional wisdom of a 60/40 equity to nonequity asset allocation for de ned bene t plans), signi cant concerns have been expressed that there will be very risk-averse employees who are unlikely to choose to invest in equities. Although this may be a proper choice for those nearing retirement age (depending on their other nancial and non nancial resources), it is likely that a majority of nancial advisors would suggest a different strategy for younger participants.

VanDerhei et al. (2008) found that more than half (50.4%) of all 401(k) participants in their 20s had none of their account balances invested in equity funds per se at the end of 2007. The number was smaller for those in their 30s but still more than a third (35.4%). However, approximately two-thirds of these participants (63.2% of those in their 20s and 69.9% of those in their 30s) have investments in company stock and/or balanced funds. Indeed, approximately one-third of these participants have life-cycle funds[12] as their only equity investment (which is typically a high-equity allocation at young ages).

IS THERE TOO MUCH EQUITY ALLOCATION FOR EMPLOYEES APPROACHING RETIREMENT AGE?

Another concern is the vulnerability of 401(k) participants to volatility in the equity markets, and this deals with extreme equity concentrations— especially for older employees. Figure 1 shows, for the year-end 2007 EBRI/ICI 401(k) database universe, the asset allocation distribution of 401(k)

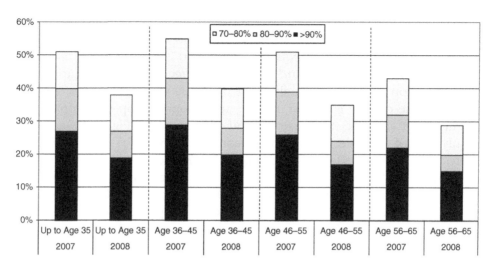

FIGURE 1 Asset allocation distribution of 401(k) participant account balances to "equity" by age: Year-end 2007 and 2008 ("equity" is de ned as equity funds + company stock + the relevant portion of balanced and target date funds). Sources: 2007: Tabulations from year-end 2007 data from EBRI/ICI Participant-Directed Retirement Plan Data Collection Project. The analysis is based on active participants with account balances at the end of 2007. 2008: Author's projections based on year-end 2007 data from EBRI/ICI Participant-Directed Retirement Plan Data Collection Project.

participant account balances to "equity" by age as of year-end 2007 and with an estimate for 2008. Equity in this gure is de ned as the percentage of the participant's 401(k) funds held in equity funds, company stock, and the equity portion of balanced and/or target-date funds.[13] The gure shows that 27% of young 401(k) participants (those 35 or younger in 2007) have 90% or more of their 401(k) assets in equities (broadly de ned). Another 13% of this cohort have 80% to 90% of their assets allocated in this fashion, and another 11% have 70% to 80% allocated to equities.

Although many asset allocation models and/or nancial advisors may suggest that extreme concentrations in equities for the young cohorts would be acceptable, few would recommend it for those approaching retirement. Nevertheless, the 2007 asset allocation information in Figure 1 shows that almost a quarter (22%) of the oldest 401(k) participants (ages 56 to 65 in 2007) had 90% or more of their 401(k) assets in equities. Another 10% had 80% to 90% in equities, and 11% had 70% to 80% in equities.

Target-date funds with automatic rebalancing and a "glide path" ensuring "age-appropriate" asset allocation are likely to become much more common after full implementation of the PPA, with an expected increase in AE for 401(k) plans and the attendant interest in QDIAs.[14] Based on unpublished EBRI research,[15] the average equity allocation for target-date funds designed for individuals in the 56 to 65 age range was 51.2% at year-end

2007. That would imply that approximately 43% of the consistent sample participants in the 56 to 65 age category would have had at least a 20 percentage point reduction in equities at year-end 2007 *if they allocated 100% to the average target-date fund for that age category.*[16] It would appear that this situation changed markedly by year-end 2008; however, it is likely that most of the change is due to market uctuations as opposed to participant transfer activity. The 2008 asset allocation estimates in Figure 1 suggest that only 15% of the oldest 401(k) participants (ages 56 to 65 in 2007) had 90% or more of their 401(k) assets in equities. Another 5% had 80% to 90% in equities, and 9% had 70% to 80% in equities. Aggregating these three categories together, the percentage of 401(k) participants aged 56 to 65 in 2007 with more than 70% of their 401(k) portfolio in equities had decreased from 43% at year-end 2007 to 29% at year-end 2008.

Is CONCENTRATION OF COMPANY STOCK A PROBLEM?

At the time of Enron's collapse, 57.73% of 401(k) plan assets were invested in company stock, which fell in value by 98.8% during 2001. The decrease in share price and eventual bankruptcy ling of Enron resulted in huge nancial losses for many of its 401(k) participants. This prompted several lawsuits as well as congressional and agency investigations into the relative bene ts and limitations of the current practice. In addition, the practice of imposing "blackout" periods when the 401(k) sponsor changes administrators was called into question in light of the Enron situation.

Certainly, the Enron situation had caused the retirement income policy community to focus increased attention to the desirability of current law and practices regarding company stock in 401(k) plans, resulting in much debate. Presumably, any recommendations to modify current pension law would attempt to strike a balance between protecting employees and not deterring employers from offering employer matches to 401(k) plans. Some have argued that if Congress were to regulate 401(k) plans too heavily, plan sponsors might choose to decrease employer contributions or not offer them at all (VanDerhei, 2002c).[17] VanDerhei and Copeland (2001) have shown that the availability and level of a company match is a primary impetus for at least some employees to make contributions to their 401(k) accounts. Others have argued that individuals should have the right to invest their money as they see t.

VanDerhei et al. (2008) indicate that the percentage of 401(k) assets in company stock decreased from 19% in 1996 and 1999 to 11% in 2007. However, when one constrains the analysis to only those plans that have company stock as either an option or a mandatory investment (in the case of an employer match), the 2007 number increases to either 18.9% or 20.5% of total 401(k) assets, depending on whether the plan also offers a guaranteed investment contract (GIC) or stable value fund.

VanDerhei et al. (2008) show that despite the marked reduction in company stock holdings in the last 10 years, there was still a potential for this investment category to be quite concentrated for some employees in 2007.[18] A total of 6.4% of participants in 401(k) plans with company stock (whether voluntary or mandatory) have more than 90% of their 401(k) balances invested in company stock, while another 8.1% have between 50% and 90% so invested. Thus, even after considerable attention in the nancial press, employer educational efforts, and legislative modi cations, 14.5% of 401(k) participants in plans offering company stock still have more than 50% of their account balances in company stock.

It is dif cult to ascertain to what extent those nondiversi ed portfolios in company stock over time are attributed to nondiversi able employer matches, inertia on the part of the employee, lack of employee understanding, signaling from the employer, or extrapolation from previous above-average returns for the company stock (Benartzi, 2001). However, it does appear that fewer new participants in the 401(k) plan are holding high concentrations in company stock. VanDerhei et al. (2008) provide annual observations from 1998[19] to 2007 of the percentages of 401(k) participants with 2 or fewer years of tenure in a 401(k) plan with company stock with (1) more than 90% of their portfolios in company stock and (2) between 50% and 90% of their portfolios in company stock.

The share of 401(k) participants in these plans with more than 90% of their account balances in company stock was 12.4% in 1998 and increased to an all-time high of 13.5% in 1999. At year-end 2001 (the best time to measure the impact of Enron on employee behavior), the level stood at 11.6%. Within a year, the value dropped to 8.4% and continued to drop each year until it was only 4.0% in 2007.

A similar phenomenon has taken place with respect to the percentage of 401(k) participants in these plans with more than 50% of their account balances in company stock. At year-end 2001, a total of 22.7% of the new participants had more than half of their balances in company stock. That number decreased to just 7.9% by year-end 2007.

IMPACT OF THE 2008–2009 MARKET CRISIS

Average Account Balances

Most of the policy concerns with respect to 401(k) participants in the last few months of 2008 focused on those close to retirement age. Figure 2 shows estimated changes in average 401(k) account balances from January 1, 2008, to June 30, 2009, broken down by age and tenure. Focusing on those on the verge of retirement (ages 56 to 65) makes it clear that the changes, to a large extent, depend on the participant's tenure with the plan sponsor. Within this group, average account balance changes varied between a positive 19% for

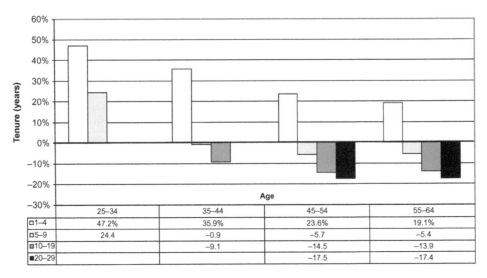

Age			
	25–34	35–44	45–54	55–64
▫1–4	47.2%	35.9%	23.6%	19.1%
▫5–9	24.4	−0.9	−5.7	−5.4
▣10–19		−9.1	−14.5	−13.9
▪20–29			−17.5	−17.4

FIGURE 2 Change in average account balances (by age and tenure) from January 1, 2008, to June 30, 2009, among 401(k) participants with account balances as of December 31, 2007. Sources: 2007 account balances: tabulations from EBRI/ICI Participant-Directed Retirement Plan Data Collection Project. 2008 and 2009 account balances: EBRI estimates. The analysis is based on all participants with account balances at the end of 2007 and contribution information for that year.

the short-tenure individuals (less than 5 years) to more than a 17% loss for those with tenure of more than 20 years.

Time for Recovery

There has been considerable discussion regarding what the current market downturn might do to retirement ages. The decision-making process undertaken by individuals or households to determine their retirement age(s) is extremely complicated, and the actual impact of a sudden drop in equity prices on retirement behavior will take years to analyze. However, as a convenient proxy for participants with a vast majority of their non–Social Security retirement wealth in 401(k) plans, Table 2 shows how long it might take for various 401(k) participants to recover the losses experienced in 2008, as a function of tenure with the current plan sponsor.[20]

Obviously, recovery times will be a function of what future market returns are assumed. Table 2 assumes a nominal annual rate of return on the nonequity portion of the portfolio of 6.3%.[21] Five different panels showing a range of returns are presented, one for each of the following equity return assumptions: −10%, −5%, 0, +5%, and +10%.[22] In addition to showing the estimated recovery time for the median individual in each tenure and equity return combination, a distributional analysis is included to show

TABLE 2 Time Needed to Recover From 2008 401(k) Losses,[a] Using Various Equity Return Assumptions and a 6.3 Percent Non-equity Return Assumption[b]

Job Tenure	Percentile of 401(k) Participants								
	10th	20th	30th	40th	Median	60th	70th	80th	90th
(years)					(years needed to recover)				
Panel A: Equity Rate of Return: −10 percent									
1–4	—	—	—	—	—	—	—	0.1	0.9
5–9	—	—	—	0.3	0.8	1.5	2.4	4.1	9.5
10–19	—	—	0.7	1.7	3.0	5.1	9.1	24.4	in nity
20–29	—	0.1	1.2	3.0	6.0	13.1	72.3	in nity	in nity
Panel B: Equity Rate of Return: −5 percent									
1–4	—	—	—	—	—	—	—	0.1	0.8
5–9	—	—	—	0.3	0.7	1.1	1.7	2.6	4.5
10–19	—	—	0.6	1.3	2.1	3.0	4.3	6.6	13.5
20–29	—	0.1	1.0	2.1	3.3	5.1	8.0	14.7	63.2
Panel C: Equity Rate of Return: 0 percent									
1–4	—	—	—	—	—	—	—	0.10	0.64
5–9	—	—	—	0.23	0.56	0.92	1.36	1.92	2.93
10–19	—	—	0.49	1.03	1.57	2.15	2.84	3.80	5.70
20–29	—	0.06	0.82	1.56	2.32	3.18	4.26	5.85	9.01
Panel D: Equity Rate of Return: +5 percent									
1–4	—	—	—	—	—	—	—	0.1	0.6
5–9	—	—	—	0.2	0.5	0.8	1.1	1.5	2.2
10–19	—	—	0.4	0.9	1.3	1.7	2.1	2.7	3.6
20–29	—	0.1	0.7	1.3	1.8	2.3	2.9	3.7	4.9
Panel E: Equity Rate of Return: +10 percent[c]									
1–4	—	—	—	—	—	—	—	0.1	0.5
5–9	—	—	—	0.2	0.4	0.7	0.9	1.3	1.7
10–19	—	—	0.4	0.7	1.1	1.4	1.7	2.1	2.6
20–29	—	0.0	0.6	1.1	1.4	1.8	2.2	2.7	3.3

Note. Source: Employee Bene t Research Institute.
[a]Losses are de ned as the difference between year-end 2007 and 2008 account balances. This is NOT limited to investment loss.
[b]"Non-equity" meaning a bond or other stable-value investment.
[c]The historic equity rate of return on equities is about 10 percent per year.

the 10th, 20th, 30th, 40th, 60th, 70th, 80th, and 90th percentiles as well. For example, the value for the 70th percentile represents a time period long enough to include the recovery times of 70% of those in the tenure and equity return combination cohort (in other words, at that value only 30% of that cohort would have recovery times greater than that amount). This additional detail is important, due to the large degree of diversity within each equity return/job tenure combination.

For example, in panel D of Table 2 (+5% equity return assumption), the *median* time to recovery for an individual in the highest job tenure category is 1.8 years. However, the 10th percentile is zero (no recovery time), due to the fact that at least 10% of the 401(k) participants in this category were estimated to have no losses in 2008,[23] and the 90th percentile is estimated to take 4.9 years before their 401(k) balances are expected to be equal to their January 1, 2008, level (in nominal terms).

A policy question that has repeatedly surfaced since the nancial market crisis began is whether the impact will be disproportionately borne by the lower-paid employees. VanDerhei (2009b) presents results for each job tenure group for six different salary groupings: $20,000 to $30,000, $30,000 to $40,000, $40,000 to $50,000, $50,000 to $60,000, $60,000 to $90,000, and greater than $90,000.[24] These ndings show that, at least for the median results, lower-paid employees will have shorter recovery times than their higher-paid counterparts, and in many cases there is a *significantly* shorter recovery time for the lowest-paid category of participants than for the highest-paid.[25]

THE FUTURE OF 401(k) PLANS

Although there have been several simulation studies attempting to project the likely retirement income produced by 401(k) plans for future cohorts of retirees, very few of them have successfully integrated two of the most important plan design changes: (1) automatic enrollment of participants coupled with automatic escalation of contributions and (2) target-date fund investments.

Would Target-Date Funds Make a Difference?

The rst portion of this section reports on the results obtained using the EBRI simulation model to determine how target-date funds would likely impact 401(k) participants who are assumed to be automatically enrolled.[26] It is important to note that target-date funds use in 401(k) plans is not limited to those automatically enrolled;[27] however, based on unpublished simulation results, it appears that 401(k) AE will represent the majority of target-date fund use in the future.

The simulation model starts with all workers, regardless of whether they are currently enrolled in 401(k) plans, and tracks them through age 65 by stochastically assigning job change, whether the new employer sponsors a 401(k) plan, cash-out behavior, and nancial market performance. In addition, the EBRI/ICI 401(k) database is used to statistically impute asset allocation under participant-directed baseline scenarios (VanDerhei et al., 2008).

Although the model produces several output metrics, the one of most interest for this discussion is the ratio of "401(k) accumulations"[28] divided by wage at the time of retirement—or, for purposes of cash-out behavior discussed later, the time of job change. The ratio of 401(k) accumulations divided by wage can be a convenient proxy for retirement security by dividing the ratio by an immediate (real) annuity purchase price at retirement age and then adding it to the percentage of preretirement income assumed to be replaced by Social Security.[29] The resulting replacement ratio can then be compared with any one of a set of previously computed thresholds to provide insight about whether the individual has adequate resources for retirement security.[30]

The following analysis focuses on the percentage increase or decrease of those balances moving from participant-directed investments to a type of investment strategy that makes use of target-date funds.[31] Target-date funds are often chosen as the default investment strategy for employees who are automatically enrolled in 401(k) plans, given that these individuals often do not exercise the effective control required for employers to bene t from the Employee Retirement Income Security Act (ERISA) Sec. 404(c) protection with respect to potential liability exposure resulting from investment losses. They put employees into asset allocations that are considered age-appropriate and then gradually decrease the equity exposure as the employees approach their target dates (typically their expected retirement dates). If one assumes a positive equity premium going forward, it is likely that employees (especially young employees) who otherwise would have chosen a relatively low-equity allocation would end up with larger 401(k) accumulations at retirement with a target-date fund as opposed to participant-directed investments. However, target-date funds for older employees who would exhibit relatively risk-averse tendencies if they invested the assets themselves may nd the higher volatility of the target-date fund results in a smaller account balance a signi cant percentage of the time (but less than 50%).[32]

Figure 3 shows the medians and interquartile range for the percentage increase in balances moving from participant direction to target-date funds. As can be seen from the medians in the middle column for each age cohort, the average impact appears to be minimal (less than 1%); however, this can be very deceiving. The 25th and 75th percentiles show that this can make a huge difference, especially for those exposed to target-date funds at a relatively young age. For those aged 25 to 29, the top 25% have at least an 8% gain, but the bottom 25% have at least a 5.9% loss.

Given the incredible range of asset allocations because of individual participant investment direction, it should not be surprising that the adoption of target-date funds has a large range of different outcomes. Figure 4 shows the same type of analysis as the previous gure, although this time only participants younger than 45 are analyzed and the relative gains are displayed as a function of the participant's initial equity allocation. Obviously, the primary advantage of target-date funds when viewed in this context is the expected gain for those with an initial low-equity allocation (of less than 30%). While some nancial advisors may argue that less than a 30% equity allocation may be optimal for those very close to retirement age, it is likely

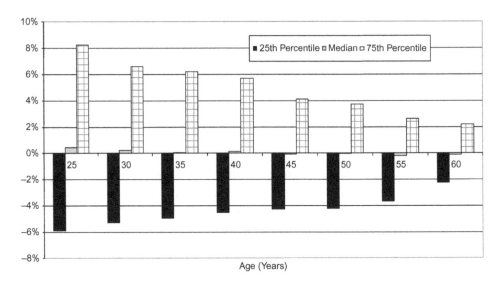

FIGURE 3 Increase in balances (401(k) and rollover IRA) at retirement age, as a function of age (average target date vs. participant direction). Source: Author's simulations based on June 16, 2009, modi cations to the EBRI/ERF Retirement Security Projection Model. For additional detail on the model, see VanDerhei and Copeland (2008).

that this will not be the case for younger participants. As can be seen in Figure 4, the positive results of target-date funds in the lower-equity alloca-tion range are much more pronounced with the 75th percentiles for those with less than a 30% allocation in the positive 25% to 37% range, while the losses associated with the 25th percentile are always less than 6%. Moreover, even the median gains in this range are in excess of 5% for all groups.

While the previous gures illustrated that target-date funds can indeed make a substantial difference in balances at retirement for some partici-pants, another concern that was often expressed (after QDIA regulations were proposed) dealt with the potential impact on participants who were likely to cash out their 401(k) balances at job change rather than roll them over to IRAs or retain them in 401(k) plans. Figure 5 shows the expected impact on these individuals of moving from participant-directed investments to target-date funds, as a function of the employee's tenure on the job. The median impact is extremely small (1% or less); however, the interquartile range increases with duration, as expected, and the 75th percentile for those with 11 or more years with the employer exceeds 6%.

Would Auto-Enrollment/Auto-Escalation Make a Difference?

As it is far too soon to analyze what percentage of 401(k) sponsors with vol-untary enrollment (VE) will adopt an AE approach, similar to VanDerhei and Copeland (2004), this analysis models the scenario in which *all* VE sponsors

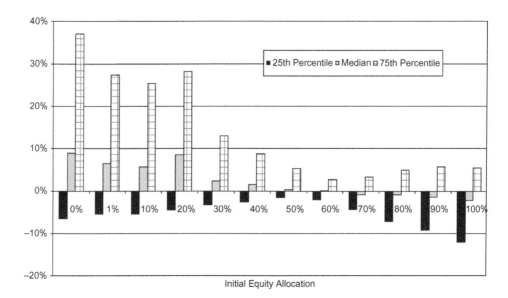

FIGURE 4 Increase in balances (401(k) and rollover IRA) at retirement age as a function of initial equity allocation (average target date vs. participant direction): participants younger than 45. Source: Author's simulations based on June 16, 2009, modi cations to the EBRI/ERF Retirement Security Projection Model. For additional detail on the model, see VanDerhei and Copeland (2008).

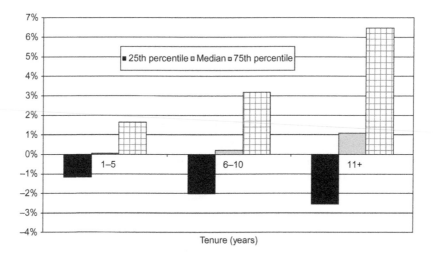

FIGURE 5 Increase in balances for those assumed to cash out when they change jobs, as a function of tenure in average target date vs. participant directed. Source: Author's simulations based on June 16, 2009, modi cations to the EBRI/ERF Retirement Security Projection Model. For additional detail on the model, see VanDerhei and Copeland (2008).

switch to AE. The results allow the users to determine the likely impact of these changes by applying whatever relative growth in the percentage of AE participants they think is most likely to occur.

The analysis in this section focuses on employees currently aged 25 to 29. This serves two purposes: (1) it indicates what the maximum impact of a change from VE to AE is likely to be in the future, and (2) it allows re nement of the results with respect to additional percentiles in the distributional analysis as well as the impact of salary and number of years participating in a 401(k) plan on the nal balances.

Table 3 provides a detailed distribution analysis of the difference between VE plans and AE plans with automatic escalation by salary quartile under the assumption of serial correlation.[33] The top panel of Table 3 pertains to the VE plans, and the next ve panels focus on the auto-escalation feature for AE plans under ve different sets of assumptions:

1. Assuming 401(k) opt-outs, limit of safe harbor minimum, start over;
2. Assuming no opt-outs, limit of safe harbor minimum, maintain contribution rates;
3. Assuming no opt-outs, limit of safe harbor maximum, maintain contribution rates;
4. Assuming 401(k) opt-outs, limit of safe harbor maximum, maintain contribution rates;
5. Assuming 401(k) opt-outs, limit of safe harbor minimum, maintain contribution rates,

where:

- *401(k) opt-outs* denote that individuals will opt out of future increases as described in the empirical ndings presented in VanDerhei (2007);
- *No opt-outs* denotes that individuals will not opt out of future increases until they reach an employer-induced constraint;
- *Safe harbor minimum* denotes that employers will limit the automatic increases to 6% of compensation;
- *Safe harbor maximum* denotes that employers will limit the automatic increases to 10% of compensation;
- *Start over* denotes that workers will start over from the default contribution when they change jobs; and
- *Maintain contribution rate* denotes that workers will retain the deferral level rate from the previous job.

Even for the most conservative set of assumptions for auto-escalation (second panel of Table 3), the AE plans result in 401(k) accumulations at least as large as the VE plans for all four salary quartiles through and including the medians. At the 75th percentile, the AE plans have higher balances

TABLE 3 Auto-Enrollment with Auto-Escalation vs. Voluntary Enrollment: Post-PPA 401(k) "Accumulations" as a Multiple of Final Earnings for Those Currently Age 25–29 (assuming future eligibility is a function of current eligibility)

Voluntary Enrollment							
Salary Quartile	5th Percentile	10th Percentile	25th Percentile	Median	75th Percentile	90th Percentile	95th Percentile
1	0	0.0	0.0	0.1	1.8	5.9	9.2
2	0	0.0	0.1	1.4	4.9	10.5	16.0
3	0	0.0	0.2	2.2	7.1	14.2	18.9
4	0	0.0	1.3	5.7	12.0	19.8	26.0
*Automatic Enrollment (assuming 401(k) opt-outs, limit of safe harbor <u>minimum, start over</u>)**							
1	0	0.0	0.2	2.5	6.5	10.3	12.9
2	0	0.0	1.0	4.0	7.6	10.9	12.5
3	0	0.0	1.7	4.7	9.0	12.4	13.9
4	0	0.5	3.0	6.2	9.5	12.6	13.9
*Automatic Enrollment (assuming no 401(k) opt-outs, limit of safe harbor <u>minimum, maintain contribution rates</u>)**							
1	0	0.0	0.3	2.8	7.1	11.2	13.2
2	0	0.1	1.8	4.8	9.1	13.0	14.2
3	0	0.4	2.6	5.9	10.2	13.2	14.6
4	0	0.3	3.3	7.3	11.3	13.8	15.1
*Automatic Enrollment (assuming no 401(k) opt-outs, limit of safe harbor <u>maximum, maintain contribution rates</u>)**							
1	0	0.0	0.4	4.5	10.4	15.5	18.4
2	0	0.0	2.4	6.6	12.1	16.6	18.2
3	0	0.0	3.1	8.0	14.0	17.7	20.5
4	0	0.9	4.9	10.0	14.7	18.1	19.8
*Automatic Enrollment (assuming 401(k) opt-outs, limit of safe harbor <u>maximum, maintain contribution rates</u>)**							
1	0	0.0	0.3	3.4	8.4	13.5	17.0
2	0	0.0	1.5	5.2	10.0	14.0	16.6
3	0	0.0	2.3	6.0	12.2	16.6	18.5
4	0	0.6	3.8	7.9	12.6	16.4	18.5
*Automatic Enrollment (assuming 401(k) opt-outs, limit of safe harbor <u>minimum, maintain contribution rates</u>)**							
1	0	0.0	0.3	2.7	7.1	11.0	13.6
2	0	0.0	1.2	4.4	8.2	11.7	13.2
3	0	0.0	1.9	5.2	9.7	13.3	15.6
4	0	0.6	3.2	6.6	10.3	13.2	14.6

Note. Source: Author's simulations.

*Terms: *401(k) opt-outs* denotes that individuals will opt out of future increases as described in the empirical ndings presented in VanDerhei (2007). *No opt-outs* denotes that individuals will not opt out of future increases until they reach an employer-induced constraint. *Safe harbor minimum* denotes that employers will limit the automatic increases to 6 percent of compensation. *Safe harbor maximum* denotes that employers will limit the automatic increases to 10 percent of compensation. *Start over* denotes that workers will start over from the default contribution when they change jobs. *Maintain contribution rate* denotes that workers will retain the deferral level rate from the previous job. Note: Post-PPA 401(k) accumulations denote retirement money at age 65 in either a 401(k) plan or IRA rollover that originated with contributions made on or after January 1, 2008.

than the VE plans for all but the highest salary quartile (again reﬂecting the often-demonstrated empirical observation that high-salary individuals do not beneﬁt as much from a higher participation rate under AE plans, and at least some of them end up with lower contribution rates for a time due to the inertia of keeping the default contribution rate—even though in this case it is assumed to be increasing annually to a 6% contribution rate). At the 90th percentile, the two lowest-salary quartiles have larger 401(k) accumulations under AE plans, but the two highest-salary quartiles do better under VE plans. At the 95th percentile, the VE plans have larger 401(k) accumulations for all but the lowest-salary quartile. For the most generous set of assumptions for auto-escalation (fourth panel of Table 3), the AE plans result in 401(k) accumulations at least as large as the VE plans for all four salary quartiles in every case, with the exception of the highest-salary quartiles for the 90th and 95th percentiles.

Other combinations of assumptions for auto-escalation result in inter-mediate results between these two extremes. Again, it will be years before researchers have enough empirical evidence to determine the relative like-lihood that any of the ﬁve AE panels would be appropriate. However, the evidence presented in Table 3 suggests that the lowest-salary quartile will always be at least as well off under AE (at least up to the 95th percentile), regardless of which set of auto-escalation assumptions proves to be cor-rect. The same can be said of the second-lowest salary quartile through the 90th percentile and the third quartile through the 75th percentile. Even the highest-salary quartile does at least as well under AE through the median regardless of the set of auto-escalation assumptions chosen.[34]

CONCLUSION

Relative to deﬁned beneﬁt plans, the importance of deﬁned contribution plans (especially 401(k) plans) has grown signiﬁcantly in recent years.[35] This paper has attempted to use administrative data from millions of 401(k) participants dating back to 1996 as well as several simulation models to determine 401(k) plans susceptibility to several alleged limitations as well as its potential for signiﬁcant retirement wealth accumulation for employees working for employers who have chosen to sponsor these plans. While participant activity during this period would certainly not be categorized as ideal, overall the data suggest that some of the more important prob-lems (such as concentration in company stock) have been signiﬁcantly improved over the last few years. The simulation models provide results under several different scenarios, but the general conclusion through the ﬁrst half of 2008 was that for those workers who participate in 401(k) plans for their entire careers, a signiﬁcant percentage of them would have retirement income (assuming the account balances were annuitized) to supplement Social Security bene ts (under the current statutory formulae) to provide a combined replacement rate that would satisfy the thresholds typically suggested to be suf cient for maintaining standard of living in retirement.

However, the current situation has changed markedly for many 401(k) participants since September 2008. This paper reviewed the large equity allocations of those close to retirement at year-end 2007 and showed that even through June 30, 2009, the average account balance for those with at least 20 years of tenure with the 401(k) sponsor decreased by 17% to 18% since year-end 2007. The length of time it will take individuals to recover from their 2008 losses varies considerably by job tenure and assumed future market returns, but even with a zero equity return assumption, the median recovery time for all groups is less than 2.5 years.

What will happen to 401(k) participants in future years will be largely determined by the extent to which the automatic features of automatic enrollment, automatic escalation of contributions, and automatic investment is allowed to play out. Simulation results suggest the rst two features will signi cantly improve retirement wealth for the lowest-income quartiles going forward, and results on the third feature (primarily target-date funds) suggest that a large percentage of those on the verge of retirement would bene t signi cantly by a reduction of equity concentrations to a more age-appropriate level.

NOTES

1. For 401(k) participants in the highest-income quartile, the median replacement rate decreased by 3.7 percentage points if the market downturn occurred at the beginning of the career. The decrease was estimated to be 10.4 percentage points if it took place at the middle of the career. If the market downturn took place at the end of the career, the estimated decrease was 17.7%. The percentage point decreases for this group were based on a median replacement rate of 67.2% of nal income, assuming a regular stochastic simulation of equity returns.

2. The EBRI/ICI Participant-Directed Retirement Plan Data Collection Project is the largest, most representative repository of information about individual 401(k) plan participant accounts. As of December 31, 2007, the EBRI/ICI database included statistical information about 21.8 million 401(k) plan participants in 56,232 employer-sponsored 401(k) plans holding $1.425 trillion in assets. The 2007 EBRI/ICI database covers 45% of the universe of 401(k) plan participants, 12% of plans, and 47% of 401(k) plan assets. The EBRI/ICI project is unique because of its inclusion of data provided by a wide variety of plan record-keepers and, therefore, portrays the activity of participants in 401(k) plans of varying sizes—from very large corporations to small businesses—with a variety of investment options. 2008 data are currently being analyzed and updates based on this information may be found at www.ebri.org.

3. The reason for the construction of this subsample is explained in the next section of the paper.

4. For purposes of this analysis, investment returns were proxied by one of the following three index returns: S&P 500 Index, Lehman Aggregate Index (and later Barclays Capital U.S. Aggregate Bond Index), or 3-month T-bills. These asset classes were assumed to have fees of 75, 45, and 45 basis points, respectively.

5. The concept of automatic escalation of employee contributions was popularized by Benartzi and Thaler (2004). However, the safe harbor provisions for AE plans under PPA have certain constraints described later in this paper.

6. There are several reasons the median values fell after 2004. Perhaps the most important is the increase in AE provisions among 401(k) plan sponsors (Choi, Laibson, & Madrian, 2004; Choi, Laibson, Madrian, & Metrick, 2005, 2006). This resulted in participants who typically did not choose to enroll voluntarily in a 401(k) plan (low-income and young employees) to participate in plans at a much higher rate. Since these individuals will start with very low balances, the medians are likely to drift to the left, ceteris paribus.

7. Currently, there is no way in which IRA rollovers can be tracked across data providers. However, beginning with year-end 2009 data, EBRI will utilize a highly secure standardized encryption algorithm that will allow these gures to be tracked and combined at least within the con nes of the database universe.

8. Note: Only a subset of the administrative data received by the data providers includes salary information. See VanDerhei et al. (2008) for additional discussion of potential sample bias introduced by this consideration.

9. For example, if a 40-year-old employee with a $100,000 account balance changed jobs and rolled the previous balance to an IRA, he or she would show up the following year as a 41-year-old employee with a much smaller account balance re ecting contributions and investment income from only a single year.

10. See VanDerhei (1983) for a more detailed account of the rst years of the 401(k) phenomenon.

11. Previous models using the EBRI/ICI data had limited the projections exclusively to current 401(k) participants and/or eligible nonparticipants.

12. A life-cycle fund typically rebalances to an increasingly conservative portfolio as the target date of the fund approaches. The likely impact of these funds on future 401(k) balances is explored later in this paper.

13. The results in this gure are not directly comparable with Figure 1 in VanDerhei (2008). In the earlier publication, equity concentrations were measured for the consistent sample of participants de ned earlier. By de nition, participants would need to be in the plan at least 7 years to be in the consistent sample. This will provide signi cant bias in the equity concentrations for the youngest cohorts.

14. The Department of Labor issued nal regulations for QDIAs on October 24, 2007, to provide, inter alia, employers who adopt AE plans a safe harbor from duciary risk when selecting an investment for participants who fail to elect their own investment. Sec. 404(c)(5)(A) of ERISA provides that, for purposes of Sec. 404(c)(1) of ERISA, a participant in an individual account plan shall be treated as exercising control over the assets in the account with respect to the amount of contributions and earnings which, in the absence of an investment election by the participant, are invested by the plan in accordance with regulations prescribed by the secretary of labor. The three types of funds speci cally enumerated for safe harbor treatment in the regulations are life-cycle (target-date) funds, balanced funds, and managed accounts.

15. This is explained in more detail in Copeland (2009).

16. It is possible that some of these participants were invested in company stock via employer matching contributions that were not able to be diversi ed.

17. VanDerhei (2002a) modeled the likely impact of restricting company stock from 401(k) plans, and VanDerhei (2002b) analyzed the potential consequences of imposing a Pension Bene t Guaranty Corporation–like insurance system against investment losses for 401(k) participants.

18. It should be noted that the EBRI/ICI 401(k) database does not contain any data on the extent to which the 401(k) participants have de ned bene t coverage. Unpublished reports at the time of Enron's collapse showed a high correlation between mandatory matching contributions in company stock and the existence of a de ned bene t plan.

19. Changes in the composition of data providers makes it problematic to include previous years on a comparable basis.

20. These losses are de ned as the difference between actual year-end 2007 and estimated 2008 account balances. It should be noted that this includes estimated contribution activity (as well as other cash ows) for 2008 and is not limited to investment losses.

21. See VanDerhei (2009b) for results when that assumption is cut in half, to a nominal return of 3.15%.

22. Some may question why any 401(k) participant would choose to continue to invest in equities if the assumed rate of return were negative. While this would certainly seem unlikely if the long-term assumptions were negative, this analysis is attempting to conduct sensitivity analysis on the possible short-term consequences of various equity return assumptions.

23. This may be due to a number of factors, but in most cases it was either a function of large contribution-to-account-balance ratios or very conservative asset allocation.

24. Participants with salaries less than $20,000 were excluded in an attempt to screen out part-time employees.

25. There are several potential explanations for this result, but the most likely is that higher-paid individuals have a higher ratio of account balances to annual contributions than do their lower-paid counterparts. This may be the result of constraints imposed by IRC Sec. 402(g), plan sponsor reactions to potential average deferral percent/average contribution percent nondiscrimination testing, or plan constraints for highly compensated employees.

26. See VanDerhei (2009a) for counterfactual evidence on how 401(k) account balances would have grown from 1999 to 2006, inclusive, had these balances been invested in three different types of target-date funds (average, aggressive, and conservative) instead.

27. Copeland (2009) provides signi cant detail on the differences.

28. This denotes both the 401(k) balances with either the current employer or previous employers that have been retained as well as any IRA balances that are attributable to 401(k) rollovers.

29. If the individual is assumed to have de ned bene t accruals at retirement, this may be added to the previous total after multiplying by the ratio of an immediate (nominal) annuity purchase price at retirement age divided by immediate (real) annuity purchase price at retirement age.

30. VanDerhei (2004) reviews how replacement rates have traditionally been used to establish minimum targets for future retirees by calculating the amount needed to provide the same amount of after-tax income in retirement as that received prior to retirement after adjusting for differences in savings, age, and work-related expenses. However, a key weakness of many retirement income models is that they use average estimates for life expectancy and, consequently, provide workers with only a 50% chance of having adequate income in retirement. VanDerhei (2006) develops a new model that incorporates a wide range of data in order to produce a far more inclusive and re ned projection of likely retirement income. In projecting retirement income needs, the new model incorporates three of the most critically important, but dif cult-to-model, retirement risks: investment risk, or how individuals' assets will perform during retirement; longevity risk, or how long an individual expects to live; and catastrophic health care costs, which have the potential to wipe out retirement savings.

31. Due to space constraints, analysis in this section is limited to the comparison of "average" target-date fund in terms of equity allocation; however, VanDerhei (2009c) includes sensitivity analysis for both the most aggressive and most conservative target-date funds as well. Although the results in this paper all assume baseline rate of return assumptions (see Park, 2009, for details), results for alternative return assumptions are provided in VanDerhei (2009c).

32. A similar situation (described below) would be expected if employees changed jobs and cashed out the 401(k) account balances within a few years of their entry date.

33. See VanDerhei and Copeland (2008) for results when future eligibility is assumed to be independent of current eligibility.

34. One public policy concern often raised, especially as the private-sector retirement system continues to evolve from de ned bene t (pension) to de ned contribution (401(k)-type) plans is the probability that a worker will end up with no 401(k) accumulations at retirement age. While many would argue that the 401(k) accumulations presented in Table 3 provide more substantive evidence of the likely overall impact of PPA on retirement income from 401(k) plans, VanDerhei and Copeland (2008) demonstrate the likely reduction of workers with no 401(k) accumulations as a result of switching from VE to AE plans. Whether one assumes serial correlation in eligibility or not, the reduction in this probability is striking, especially for the lowest-salary quartile. If future eligibility is assumed to be a function of current eligibility as parameterized in this section, the probability of having no 401(k) balance for this group drops from 41% to 24% by switching from VE to AE. If serial correlation is ignored, the difference is even greater, dropping from 40% to 16%.

35. Copeland and VanDerhei (2009) investigate how the role of private de ned bene t pension plans has declined since the advent of ERISA in 1974. Even including public-sector retirees, Americans with de ned bene t plan incomes never reached 40% of the retiree population and the fraction has receded several percentage points from its highest levels in the early 1990s. Of course, these historical gures do not re ect the considerable recent activity in de ned bene t freezes for new (and sometimes existing) employees since 2006.

REFERENCES

Benartzi, S. (2001). Excessive extrapolation and the allocation of 401(k) accounts to company stock? *Journal of Finance, 56*(5), 1747–1764.

Benartzi, S., & Thaler, R. H. (2004). Save more tomorrow: Using behavioral economics to increase employee saving. *Journal of Political Economy, 112*(1), S164–S182.

Choi, J. J., Laibson, D. I., & Madrian, B. C. (2004). Plan design and 401(k) savings outcomes. *NBER Working Paper*, No. W10486.

Choi, J. J., Laibson, D. L., Madrian, B. C., & Metrick, A. (2005). Optimal defaults and active decisions. *NBER Working Paper*, No. 11074.

Choi, J. J., Laibson, D. L., Madrian, B. C., & Metrick, A. (2006). Saving for retirement on the path of least resistance. In E. McCaffrey & J. Slemrod (Eds.), *Behavioral public finance: Toward a new agenda* (pp. 304–351). New York: Russell Sage Foundation.

Copeland, C. (2009). Use of target-date funds in 401(k) plans, 2007. *EBRI Issue Brief*, 327 (Employee Bene t Research Institute).

Copeland, C., & VanDerhei, J. (2009). *The declining role of private defined benefit pension plans: Who is affected, and how*. Pension Research Council Working Paper WP2009-18.

Holden, S., & VanDerhei, J. (2001). 401(k) plan asset allocation, account balances, and loan activity in 2000. *EBRI Issue Brief, 239 and ICI Perspective* (Employee Bene t Research Institute and Investment Company Institute).

Holden, S., & VanDerhei, J. (2002). Can 401(k) accumulations generate signi cant income for future retirees? *EBRI Issue Brief*, 251 and *ICI Perspective* (Employee Bene t Research Institute and Investment Company Institute).

Holden, S., & VanDerhei, J. (2005). The in uence of automatic enrollment, catch-up, and IRA contributions on 401(k) accumulations at retirement. *EBRI Issue Brief*, 283 and *ICI Perspective* (Employee Bene t Research Institute and Investment Company Institute).

Park, Y. (2009). Plan demographics, participants' saving behavior, and target-date fund investments. *EBRI Issue Brief*, 329 (Employee Bene t Research Institute).

VanDerhei, J. (1983). Section 401(k) plans and thrift plans. In J. S. Rosenbloom (Ed.), *Employee benefits handbook* (pp. 496–516). Homewood, IL: Dow Jones-Irwin.

VanDerhei, J. (2002a). The role of company stock in 401(k) plans. *Risk Management and Insurance Review, 5*(1), 20.

VanDerhei, J. (2002b). *Picking up the Enron pieces*. Written statement for the Senate Finance Committee Hearing on Retirement Security, February 27.

VanDerhei, J. (2002c). Company stock in 401(k) plans: Results of ISCEBS members. *Benefits Quarterly*, 65–76.

VanDerhei, J. (2004). Measuring retirement income adequacy, part one: Traditional replacement ratios and results for workers at large companies. *EBRI Notes*, 9 (Employee Bene t Research Institute), 2–12.

VanDerhei, J. (2006). Measuring retirement income adequacy: Calculating realistic income replacement rates. *EBRI Issue Brief*, 297 (Employee Bene t Research Institute).

VanDerhei, J. (2007). The expected impact of automatic escalation of 401(k) contributions on retirement income. *EBRI Notes*, 9, 1–8.

VanDerhei, J. (2008). *The impact of the financial crisis on workers' retirement security*. Testimony before the House Education and Labor Committee. October.

VanDerhei, J. (2009a). *Frozen pensions and falling stocks: What will happen to retirees' incomes?* Urban Institute Presentation (February 3).

VanDerhei, J. (2009b). The impact of the recent nancial crisis on 401(k) account balances. *EBRI Issue Brief*, 326 (Employee Bene t Research Institute).

VanDerhei, J. (2009c). *How would target-date funds likely impact future 401(k) accumulations?* Working paper available at SSRN: http://ssrn.com/abstract=1422726.

VanDerhei, J., & Copeland, C. (2001). A behavioral model for predicting employee contributions to 401(k) plans. *North American Actuarial Journal* (First Quarter).

VanDerhei, J., & Copeland, C. (2004). ERISA at 30: The decline of private-sector de ned bene t promises and annuity payments: What will it mean? *EBRI Issue Brief*, 269 (Employee Bene t Research Institute).

VanDerhei, J., & Copeland, C. (2008). The impact of PPA on retirement income for 401(k) participants. *EBRI Issue Brief*, 318 (Employee Bene t Research Institute).

VanDerhei, J., Galer, R., Quick, C., & Rea, J. D. (1999). 401(k) plan asset allocation, account balances, and loan activity. *EBRI Issue Brief*, 205 and *ICI Perspective* (Employee Bene t Research Institute and Investment Company Institute).

VanDerhei, J., Holden, S., Alonso, L., & Copeland, C. (2008). 401(k) plan asset allocation, account balances, and loan activity in 2007. *EBRI Issue Brief*, 324 and *ICI Perspective* (Employee Bene t Research Institute and Investment Company Institute).

Did Retirees Save Enough to Compensate for the Increase in Individual Risk Exposure?

CHRISTIAN E. WELLER, PhD

Associate Professor, Department of Public Policy and Public Affairs, University of Massachusetts Boston, Boston, Massachusetts, USA, and Senior Fellow, Center for American Progress, Washington, DC, USA

The United States experienced an unprecedented financial crisis after 2007. This paper analyzes whether retirees had enough wealth built up to weather the financial risks that materialized in the crisis. Financial risks associated with saving for retirement had increasingly shifted onto individuals and away from the public and employers during the decades before the crisis. This growing personal responsibility should have brought about more saving and less risk taking. I use data from the Federal Reserve's triennial Survey of Consumer Finances first to define an income threshold for retirees, specifically whether annuity income is greater than twice the poverty line: a common proxy for basic income needs. I then calculate the potential retirement income that retirees could expect if they translated all of their wealth into income and if the income is adjusted for market, idiosyncratic, and longevity risks. I compare the potential risk-adjusted income for retirees with annuity income above twice the poverty line to those retirees with annuity income below twice the poverty line. Both groups of retirees should have at least the same level of risk-adjusted potential retirement income. This comparison shows, however, that retirees with annuity income below twice the poverty line did not build up sufficient wealth to compensate for the rising financial risk exposure. Public policy thus should maintain existing sources of annuity income, promote greater annuitization of financial wealth, and encourage additional savings.

INTRODUCTION

The nancial crisis after 2007 created an unprecedented drop in personal wealth. Did retirees have enough of a nancial cushion to withstand the fallout from the crisis without a drop in living standards? Individuals had to take more responsibility for saving for their retirement during the decades before the crisis and thus became increasingly exposed to the kind of nancial market risks that materialized after 2007. On the other hand, the greater risk exposure was meant to give individuals an added incentive to save more for retirement. They therefore may have built up more of a nancial cushion for a potential crisis than they otherwise would have. Household wealth, after all, increased relative to income during the decades before the crisis.

Most researchers, though, conclude that despite sharp increases in wealth, a substantial number of families were still ill-prepared for retirement and that younger cohorts were increasingly less likely to be able to maintain their standard of living in retirement. This apparent contradiction between rising wealth and falling retirement income security may result from the fact that analyses of retirement income adequacy rely on measures of wealth that are not adjusted for the changing risk exposure of individuals over time.

My analysis researches whether the shift toward more personal responsibility went along with suf ciently larger personal wealth to compensate for the concomitant increase in individual risk exposure. I consider the potential retirement income of two groups of retirees: those who receive annuities from pensions and Social Security that are at least twice as great as the poverty line and thus have their basic living expenses covered and those who do not. I look at the potential income that both groups of retirees could expect to receive from all sources, including their wealth, after adjusting for the risks embedded in their wealth. If the shift toward more personal responsibility improved retirement income security, the risk-adjusted potential retirement income of retirees with annuity income below twice the poverty line should be at least as large as the risk-adjusted potential retirement income of retirees with annuity income above twice the poverty line. If this is not the case, the shift toward more personal responsibility has gone along with a decline in retirement income security and requires policy attention to boost retirement income security after personal wealth has dropped dramatically.

My research adds to the existing literature in several ways. First, I explicitly account for individual risk exposure of retirees in calculating potential retirement income, instead of assuming many risks away. Second, I analyze the potential retirement incomes of current retirees instead of forecasting expected retirement incomes for future retirees, thus eliminating several sources of uncertainty about retirement income security. Third, I extend the research on retirement income adequacy to include data through 2007 to get a sense of how retirement income security changed just before the crisis occurred.

This paper is organized as follows: a discussion of the relevant literature, followed by a presentation of some summary statistics. I then present the concept of and data on risk-adjusted potential retirement income, followed by the multivariate regression analyses for retiree risk exposure, wealth, and income security. Concluding remarks contain a discussion of the policy implications.

LITERATURE REVIEW

Retirement income adequacy is commonly de ned as a minimum threshold (typically 75% to 80%) of the ratio of potential retirement income from Social Security, pensions, and private savings to pre-retirement income (Henle, 1972; Engen, Gale, & Uccelo, 1999; RETIRE Project, 2001). The income needs of retirees are likely to be lower than those of workers since retirees no longer need to save for retirement, pay fewer taxes, have no work-related expenses, have smaller families, and often do not have mortgages (Engen et al., 1999). The target replacement rate, though, can vary with pre-retirement income levels and family status (CRR, 2006).

Most research nds that typically between 35% and 50% of U.S. work-ers cannot meet the replacement rate (Bernheim, 1997; Engen et al., 1999; Gustman & Steinmeier, 1999; Moore & Mitchell, 2000; Munnell, Golub-Sass, & Webb, 2007; Weller & Wolff, 2005). Expressed slightly differently, U.S. workers are saving only a fraction—a third or less—of what they would need to save for adequate retirement income (Bernheim, 1997; Moore & Mitchell, 2000). These ndings still hold when only retirees are considered, instead of projecting future retirement income for current workers (Munnell & Soto, 2005).

An alternative approach to retirement income adequacy is the compar-ison of expected retirement income to an absolute standard, such as the poverty line or twice the poverty line (Butrica, Murphy, & Zedlewski, 2007; Haveman, Holden, Wolfe, & Romanov, 2005; Love, Smith, & McNair, 2008; Weller & Wolff, 2005). For instance, about 30% of near-retiree families in 2001 were expected to fall short of having retirement income at least equal to twice the poverty line (Weller & Wolff, 2005), which can serve as a proxy for basic living standards (Russell, Bruce, & Conahan, 2006).

Studies on retirement income adequacy typically eliminate substantial individual risk exposures in their calculations by assuming that retirees will purchase in ation-adjusted annuities with their private wealth upon retirement.

Typically, though, retirees do not annuitize their savings (Perun, 2007), which means that the risk exposures of retirees have risen over time since the dependence on wealth that is automatically annuitized has declined. Fewer private sector workers, for instance, have de ned bene t pensions and more have de ned contribution plans (EBSA, 2008; BLS, 2008).

This shift has increasingly exposed retirees to longevity, market, and idiosyncratic risks. Longevity risk could be reduced through lifetime annu-ities, but the vast majority of retirees do not annuitize their savings, even when given the chance (Perun, 2007). Moreover, savers can only reach a lim-ited protection from market risks through diversi cation of their assets. And savers may fall prey to idiosyncratic risks. Savers must make contribution, investment, and withdrawal choices by themselves in de ned contribution plans, with a high chance of making the wrong choice (Benartzi & Thaler, 2007; Englehart, 1999; Hurd & Panis, 2006; Mitchell & Utkus, 2004; Munnell & Sunden, 2004).

There is theoretically a positive link between greater risk exposure and more saving. The rationale is that individuals save more to build a cushion against the possibility that the growing risks will materialize (Browning & Lusardi, 1996; Carroll & Samwick, 1998; Holst, 2005).

Researchers have similarly analyzed whether the shift from de ned ben-e t to de ned contribution plans has resulted in more saving, but there is no clear conclusion in the literature. Papke (1999) concludes that de ned con-tribution plans merely replace de ned bene t plans without a net gain in personal retirement savings, Engen and Gale (2000) show that there are lim-ited positive savings effects for low-income savers, and Benartzi and Thaler (2007) conclude that increases in tax incentives resulted in lower contribu-tion rates since savers relied on heuristics rather than individual optimization. In comparison, Poterba, Rauh, Venti, and Wise (2007) and Poterba, Venti, and Wise (2007) nd a positive effect on personal saving, especially among higher-income earners.

The growing risk exposure should also have gone along with risk reduction strategies such as asset diversi cation and declining leverage in personal wealth. The data, though, indicate that the opposite has been the case. For instance, de ned contribution plan participants do not opti-mally diversify across asset classes, often because choices are too complex (Benartzi & Thaler, 2007; Huberman & Jiang, 2006; Iyengar & Kamenica, 2006), they hold a relatively high share of their assets in their employer's stock (Benartzi & Thaler, 2007; Holden, VanDerhei, Alonso, & Copeland, 2008; Fidelity Investments, 2009), and they only infrequently rebalance their portfolios (Mitchell, Mottola, & Utkus, 2005; Reid & Holden, 2008). Furthermore, leverage has generally increased among U.S. families (Weller & Sabatini, 2008).

Shifting the focus from all households to retirees, conclusions on the savings of retirees depend on the types of retirement plans by which they are covered. Retirees with de ned bene t plans tend to have more wealth than those with de ned contribution plans (Copeland, 2007; Love, Smith, & McNair, 2007). The risk exposure of retirees also seems to have increased with the shift from de ned bene t to de ned contribution plans (Copeland, 2006; Munnell & Sunden, 2004; VanDerhei, Holden, Alonso, & Copeland, 2008; Weller, 2009). I will thus investigate whether savings have increased enough, if at all, to compensate for the increasing risk exposure of retirees.

DESCRIPTIVE STATISTICS

My sample comprises retirees 55 years of age and older from the Federal Reserves' triannual data Survey of Consumer Finances (SCF) (BOG, 2009a). The SCF includes comprehensive information on household wealth for every third year from 1989 to 2007.

I separate retirees into those who are exposed to more risks and those who are exposed to fewer risks. I use the level of annuity income from pensions and Social Security as an indicator for the level of risk exposure. Even though Social Security is expected to encounter nancial shortfalls in the long run, proposals for Social Security reform typically exempt workers and retirees 55 and older from any changes. In a similar vein, although pension bene ts could theoretically change due to an employer's bankruptcy, bene ts are insured, within limits, by the Pension Bene t Guaranty Corporation. It is thus reasonable to consider pension and Social Security incomes of current retirees as risk-free. I then de ne a household as income secure if its annuity income is at least as large as twice the poverty line. Retirees with annuity income of at least twice the poverty line should have less wealth and possibly face more risks with their wealth than retirees with annuity income below twice the poverty line.

Table 1 summarizes trends on pension and Social Security income. Only 37.1% of retirees had annuity incomes above twice the poverty line in 2007, down from 43.7% in 2004. This decline after 2004 likely re ects broader economic trends and suggests that the deterioration in income security for retirees may have continued after 2007. The earlier increase before 2004 was likely a result of higher Social Security bene ts that followed a strong labor market in the late 1990s and of solid pension bene ts due to an extended stock market run (Weller & Wolff, 2005). The decline from 2004 to 2007 similarly may have coincided with fewer Social Security bene ts due to an especially weak labor market, cuts to Social Security bene ts for new retirees starting in 2002, and a wave of pension freezes, following funding uncertainty due to large economic, nancial market, and legal changes (Munnell, Golub-Sass, Soto, & Vitagliano, 2006).

TABLE 1 Amounts and Income Shares of Annuitized Retiree Income, 1989 to 2007

	1989	1992	1995	1998	2001	2004	2007
Median real annuitized income for households with annuitized income	$18,626	$16,317	$18,001	$18,045	$18,034	$21,428	$20,594
Median share of annuitized income out of total income for households with annuitized income	60.0	60.0	61.5	61.2	59.4	71.4	73.2
Annuitized income exceeds twice the poverty line, all households	8.8	24.9	25.9	31.2	33.1	43.7	37.1
Total wealth to income for households with annuity income above twice the poverty line	408.0	518.3	535.6	423.9	500.7	578.7	558.7
Total wealth to income for households with annuity income below twice the poverty line	579.3	558.9	437.8	473.1	610.7	404.1	472.1
Equities out of nancial assets for households with nancial investments and annuity income above twice the poverty line	28.1	22.3	26.8	42.3	53.3	48.3	33.8
Equities out of nancial assets for households with nancial investments and with annuity income below twice the poverty line	26.7	28.6	41.2	42.0	52.0	41.7	42.9
Median debt to income for retirees with debt and with annuity income above twice the poverty line	28.8	31.0	21.4	46.5	43.9	41.5	46.6
Median debt to income for retirees with debt and with annuity income below twice the poverty line	27.4	22.0	33.2	44.8	32.4	59.9	77.6

Note. Due to the survey design, shares of income can theoretically be greater than 100% but are capped at 100%. All nancial variables reference the entire household. All gures are percentages unless otherwise speci ed. Author's calculations based on BOG (2009a).

Next, Table 1 compares wealth between retirees with annuity incomes above twice the poverty line and those without. I report total wealth relative to income to control for wealth differences that occur as a result of different income levels.[1] There is no clear trend in differences of the wealth to income ratio by the level of annuity income.

The other side of income security is risk exposure, also shown in Table 1. I use the share of equities out of nancial assets as an indicator of nancial asset diversi cation and debt levels as an indicator of leverage. There is, again, no systematic difference in equity shares and debt levels by annuity income levels.

INCOME REPLACEMENT BY RETIREES

My primary goal is to estimate the ability of retirees to maintain their standards of living even if nancial risks materialize. I rst calculate the risk-adjusted potential income that retirees could expect to generate from their wealth and then compare this potential retirement income to actual non-annuity income of retirees.

My calculation of risk-adjusted potential retirement income captures the spirit of previous retirement income adequacy studies since it accounts for all potential sources of retirement income, except earnings.[2] The differences to previous research, though, are that I consider only retirees and thus do not have to forecast wealth to the time of retirement and that I explicitly account for the nancial risk exposure in private assets instead of assuming it away. The result is a more accurate measure of retiree income security.

All marketable wealth is converted to potential risk-adjusted income. Marketable wealth is the sum of housing and non-housing wealth. I rst determine the potential risk-adjusted income that retirees could receive from their owner-occupied housing. Potential income from living in an owner-occupied home is typically encapsulated in the user costs of a homeowner, what an owner-occupied property would cost in the rental market.[3] The basic calculation is de ned by:

$$user \cos t_t = P_t^h(i_t + \gamma - E\pi_t^h) \tag{1}$$

where P is the current price of the home; i is the mortgage rate; γ is the sum of depreciation, maintenance and repair, insurance, and property tax rates, which are all assumed to be constant and sum to 7%; and π is the 1-year home price appreciation; and E is an expectations operator. Data on house values are from the SCF; the mortgage rate is the average annual rate during the survey year (BOG, 2009b); and the expected home price appreciation is equal to the average annual growth rate of the Home Price Index from the Of ce of Federal Housing Enterprise Oversight (OFHEO, 2009) during the preceding 15 years.

I also convert non-housing wealth—non-housing assets minus non-mortgage debt—into potential income using a risk-free real interest rate. This calculates the amount of annual income that retirees could expect from their wealth if the money were invested in risk-free assets and increased with in ation each year. I use the 10-year average real interest rate for treasury bonds with 10 years of maturity for the calculation of the risk-free interest rate and subtract the 10-year average in ation rate based on the Consumer Price Index Research Series Using Current Methods (BLS, 2009). Moreover, I assume that retirees will not annuitize their wealth and thus have to plan for their maximum life expectancy instead of the average life expectancy as would be the case if all wealth were annuitized. The maximum life expectancy is de ned as 90 years for households younger than 90 years, 100 years for households between the ages of 90 and 99, and 105 years for households over the age of 100. The use of a real risk-free interest rates accounts for market and idiosyncratic risks, while the use of a maximum life expectancy instead of an average life expectancy accounts for longevity risk.

Total risk-adjusted potential income is the sum of annuity income, transfer income, real user costs of homes, and the real potential conversion value of non-housing wealth.[4]

Table 2 summarizes the data on risk-adjusted potential retiree income. It shows the total risk-adjusted potential retiree income and it shows the non-annuity potential retiree income relative to discretionary income. I de ne discretionary as total income minus annuity income. The ratio of non-annuity potential income to discretionary income assumes that current income is equal to desired income. I thus de ne income security as maintaining the current level of consumption.

The data in Table 2 suggest that retirees with annuity incomes above twice the poverty line also enjoy greater overall income security than other retirees. The data show that retirees with basic income security have higher risk-adjusted potential incomes than retirees without basic income security. This largely re ects the fact that retirees with basic income security tend to have more absolute wealth than retirees without basic income security. A substantial minority of retirees also were unable to maintain their current levels of income if they also wanted to protect themselves from market, idiosyncratic, and longevity risks. Thirty-four percent of retirees with annuity income above twice the poverty line and 51.1% of retirees with less annuity income were unable in 2007 to replace their discretionary income with their potential risk-adjusted retirement income. Retirees with basic income security are better situated than their counterparts to maintain or even increase their current retirement incomes, although large shortfalls remain.[5]

The gures also indicate that there is substantial variability in the levels of income security for retirees. The last peak of income security was typically 2001 for both groups of retirees. Retirement income adequacy thus had fallen even before the crisis occurred and likely left many retirees vulnerable to potential reductions in their retirement consumption.

TABLE 2 Summary Data on Retirement Income Security, 1989 to 2007

	1989	1992	1995	1998	2001	2004	2007
Real risk-adjusted potential income of retirees with annuity income above twice the poverty line	$58,398	$61,032	$67,573	$63,459	$76,502	$76,215	$70,830
Real risk-adjusted potential income of retirees with annuity incomes below twice the poverty line	$32,553	$24,698	$25,981	$27,768	$28,227	$26,929	$30,249
Risk-adjusted potential income minus annuity income relative to discretionary income for retirees with annuity income above twice the poverty line	102.0	122.6	129.8	132.3	136.3	131.4	118.2
Risk-adjusted potential income minus annuity income relative to discretionary income for retirees with annuity income below twice the poverty line	98.9	83.3	80.2	86.9	96.8	96.4	99.3
Share of retirees with annuity income above twice the poverty line whose potential income minus annuity income is smaller than their discretionary income.	48.7	33.2	30.8	30.7	27.7	30.0	34.5
Share of retirees with annuity income below twice the poverty line whose potential income minus annuity income is smaller than their discretionary income	51.4	58.1	57.4	55.6	53.3	54.2	51.0

Note. All gures are percentages unless otherwise noted. Absolute and relative risk-adjusted real amounts of potential income are medians. Shares of households are averages. Author's calculations based on BOG (2009a).

MULTIVARIATE ANALYSIS

The descriptive statistics indicate that retirees with annuity incomes greater than twice the poverty level tend to be better positioned to maintain their standards of living throughout their retirement than other retirees. Much of this difference is likely explained by demographic differences and variation in savings attitudes. I consequently estimate multivariate regressions for retirement income security. The dependent variables are the natural logarithms of the total real potential income and the difference between risk-adjusted potential income and annuity income to discretionary income: the primary income replacement variable of interest in my research. The explanatory variables are demographic characteristics—race, family status, income, and age—and personal savings characteristics—willingness to take risks as well as homeownership.

In addition, I include an indicator variable for basic income security in the regression analyses. It takes the value of "1" if annuity income from pensions and Social Security is at least twice as great as the poverty line and "0" otherwise. I alternatively use an indicator variable that takes the value of "1" if annuity income is at least as great as the poverty line to test for the robustness of my results and the continuous ratio of annuity income relative to total retiree income. These variables should have no or a negative systematic effect on the absolute or relative retirement income security if families compensate for greater nancial risk exposures by saving more and investing in more secure assets. A positive coef cient, on the other hand, would imply that retirees did not fully compensate for increased nancial risk exposures over the previous decades and thus likely experienced greater retirement income security during the period of nancial and economic turmoil after 2007.

My sample includes retirees 55 years old and older and excludes households with potential incomes less than zero or greater than $2 million, as well as those with ratios of potential income minus annuity income relative to discretionary income that are greater than 700% to avoid that the results are in uenced by outliers. My results are not sensitive to these restrictions.

Table 3 summarizes the estimates for the determinants of real risk-adjusted potential income. All coef cients have the expected signs or are statistically insigni cant. My results show that retirement income security tends to be lower for minorities, single women, families with less educational attainment than their counterparts, households with lower risk tolerances, and renters.

The important explanatory variable in the regressions presented in Table 3 is the indicator variable for annuity income above twice the poverty line. This indicator variable is statistically signi cant and positively related to absolute and relative retirement income security. This indicates that retirees with annuity incomes above twice the poverty line are more likely than other retirees to maintain their overall standards of living throughout retirement, even if nancial risks materialize. This implies that retiree self-insurance has not worked as expected.

Retirement income security may have deteriorated over time. Older retirees have more risk-adjusted potential incomes than younger ones, which could signal that retirement income security may deteriorate in the future as retirees who cannot rely as much on annuity income as previous cohorts enter retirement. Additionally, the estimates for the real values and for the

TABLE 3 Regression Results for Determinants of Potential Income, 1989 to 2007

Variable	Dependent variable: real potential income (natural logarithm)			Dependent variable: potential income minus annuity income to discretionary income		
	Annuity income above twice the poverty line	Annuity income above the poverty line	Annuity income as share of total income	Annuity income above twice the poverty line	Annuity income above the poverty line	Annuity income as share of total income
Black	−0.304***	−0.230***	−0.352***	−0.228***	−0.181***	−0.304***
	(0.046)	(0.048)	(0.050)	(0.049)	(0.052)	(0.048)
Hispanic	−0.360***	−0.344***	−0.434***	−0.140	−0.131	−0.191*
	(0.101)	(0.097)	(0.103)	(0.108)	(0.108)	(0.105)
Other race	−0.233	−0.222	−0.274	−0.013	−0.007	−0.090
	(3.317)	(3.317)	(3.317)	(3.318)	(3.318)	(3.317)
Less than high school	−0.796***	−0.869***	−0.953***	−0.201***	−0.251***	−0.391***
	(0.039)	(0.038)	(0.041)	(0.064)	(0.061)	(0.060)
High school	−0.484***	−0.566***	−0.592***	−0.041	−0.097**	−0.160***
	(0.033)	(0.033)	(0.035)	(0.051)	(0.048)	(0.046)
Some college	−0.260***	−0.320***	−0.314***	−0.006	−0.046	−0.083
	(0.041)	(0.042)	(0.044)	(0.068)	(0.066)	(0.063)
Single women	−0.149***	−0.193***	−0.249***	−0.169**	−0.199**	−0.210***
	(0.043)	(0.042)	(0.045)	(0.078)	(0.080)	(0.079)
Married	0.306***	0.333***	0.270***	−0.117	−0.100	−0.079
	(0.044)	(0.042)	(0.045)	(0.077)	(0.079)	(0.079)
Age	0.077***	0.061*	0.109***	−0.012	0.022	−0.073*
	(0.030)	(0.031)	(0.032)	(0.040)	(0.039)	(0.039)
Age^2	−0.0004**	−0.0003	−0.001***	0.0003	0.0002	0.001***
	(0.0002)	(0.0002)	(0.0002)	(0.0003)	(0.0003)	(0.0003)
Homeowner	0.657***	0.644***	0.680***	0.039	0.030	−0.055
	(0.072)	(0.070)	(0.075)	(0.100)	(0.100)	(0.099)
Risk attitude	−0.202***	−0.227***	−0.240***	−0.066**	−0.083***	−0.150***
	(0.021)	(0.022)	(0.023)	(0.032)	(0.032)	(0.030)

	(1)	(2)	(3)	(4)	(5)	(6)
Has annuity income above twice the poverty line	0.558*** (0.025)			0.372*** (0.051)		0.825*** (0.080)
Has annuity income above the poverty line		0.510*** (0.031)			0.331*** (0.032)	
Annuity income as share of total income			0.033 (0.046)			
1992	−0.273*** (0.052)	−0.372*** (0.055)	−0.183*** (0.053)	−0.139** (0.069)	−0.202*** (0.070)	−0.073 (0.067)
1995	−0.293*** (0.056)	−0.394*** (0.057)	−0.213*** (0.056)	−0.139** (0.071)	−0.204*** (0.070)	−0.096 (0.066)
1998	−0.213*** (0.051)	−0.287*** (0.055)	−0.093* (0.053)	−0.051 (0.082)	−0.098 (0.080)	0.031 (0.074)
2001	−0.113** (0.050)	−0.219*** (0.055)	0.010 (0.051)	−0.052 (0.077)	−0.119 (0.075)	−0.004 (0.070)
2004	−0.139*** (0.050)	−0.208*** (0.053)	0.038 (0.051)	−0.105 (0.078)	−0.146* (0.079)	−0.056 (0.076)
2007	−0.146*** (0.055)	−0.234*** (0.059)	−0.002 (0.055)	−0.107 (0.070)	−0.162** (0.070)	−0.068 (0.066)
Constant	7.755*** (1.129)	4.921*** (1.194)	6.869*** (1.201)	0.598 (1.414)	1.051 (1.371)	3.049** (1.378)
N	3,497	3,497	3,497	3,497	3,497	3,497
Adjusted R^2	0.517	0.513	0.424	0.148	0.138	0.221

Note. All demographic variables refer to the head of household. Risk attitude measures a household's willingness to take nancial risks on a 4-point scale where a lower number indicates a greater willingness to take nancial risks. Regression results derive from a population-weighted regression. The results are robust for unweighted regressions. Missing reference variables are "White," "college," "single men," "renter," and "1989." Author's calculations based on BOG (2009a).
*Indicates signi cance at the 1% level; **indicates signi cance at the 5% level; and ***indicates signi cance at the 10% level.

replacement values of discretionary retiree income with annuity income at the poverty level as the threshold show that retirement income security in 2007 was below the levels of 2004 and 2001.

Are the differences in retirement income security for the two groups of retirees due to too little wealth, too much risk, or both? The next regressions test the relationship among wealth, risks, and annuity income. The wealth regression uses the ratio of total marketable wealth to income as the dependent variable.[6] The explanatory variables are the same as before. The expectation is that the indicator variable for annuity income above twice the poverty line is negatively related with total wealth, suggesting that greater risk exposure leads to more wealth.

The regressions to test for risk reintroduce risks that had been eliminated in the calculations before in the calculation of risk-free potential retirement income, speci cally longevity, market, and idiosyncratic risks. I eliminated longevity risk by assuming that assets will be drawn down over a maximum life expectancy. I now reintroduce longevity risk by assuming that retirees will draw down their nancial wealth over their average life expectancy. I also eliminated market and idiosyncratic risks by discounting nancial wealth by the risk-free real interest rate and assuming that retirees will live in their homes and not sell them. I now allow for market and idiosyncratic risk exposure by assuming that retirees will have to generate market rates of return on all of their wealth. This implies that retirees are selling their homes to pay for their living expenses. The market rates of return for equities are the real total rate of return on the S&P 500, the real interest rate on the 10-year treasury for non-equity nancial wealth, and the real appreciation rate of owner-occupied housing based on OFHEO's House Price Index, all averaged over 15 years.

The new risky dependent variables follow the model of the earlier dependent variable and are set relative to current discretionary income. The indicator variable for annuity income above twice the poverty line should have a negative relationship with the potential retirement income that allows for longevity or market risk exposure, just as before. Such a negative relationship would imply that retirees who have annuity incomes below twice the poverty line also have more private wealth, albeit with an increased nancial risk exposure than other retirees.

An important additional aspect of my analysis is the change in the estimated parameter for the annuity income indicator. If the estimated difference shrinks after allowing for longevity risk, it would imply that retirees with annuity income below twice the poverty line are exposed to more longevity risk, largely because they are younger. A similar logic applies to the difference in market risk exposure. If retirees with annuity incomes below twice the poverty line are exposed to less market risk than other retirees, the reintroduction of market risks should widen the estimated gap in risk-exposed retirement income compared to risk-adjusted income. Allowing for greater risk exposure than before means that families will have to set aside less money to protect themselves from the chance that risks will materialize and thus have more retirement income available. This effect is greater for the group of families that faces more risks.

The rst regression in Table 4 shows the estimates for total wealth to income. All variables have the expected signs or are statistically insigni cant. The results show that retirees with annuity income below twice the poverty line have more wealth relative to income, as expected.

This difference in wealth, though, is not enough to provide retirees who have annuity incomes below twice the poverty line with the same ability to maintain their standards of living as other retirees. The second and third regressions in Table 4 show that retirees with annuity incomes above twice the poverty line still enjoy greater retirement income security. The second regression, which allows for longevity risk exposure, shows that allowing for the annuitization of nancial wealth shrinks the gap between the two groups of retirees. For the average retiree with annuity income above twice the poverty line, the ratio of risk-adjusted potential retirement income minus annuity income to discretionary income is 37.2 percentage points greater than for other retirees. The difference shrinks to 21.1 percentage points when I allow for longevity risk exposure. Reducing the longevity risk exposure for retirees through annuitization of their nancial wealth could thus substantially improve retirement income security.

The third regression shows the estimates after allowing for market and idiosyncratic risk exposure. Retirees with annuity incomes above twice the poverty line still enjoy more overall retirement income security than other retirees. The policy implication is thus that retirees with annuity incomes below twice the poverty line did not build up enough wealth to compensate for their remaining market risk exposures. Moreover, the difference in income security between these two groups widens when market risk is allowed, compared to the previous results, suggesting that retirees with annuity incomes above twice the poverty line are more exposed to market risks than other retirees, as the fth regression in Table 4 con rms.

CONCLUSION

In this paper, I analyze income security for U.S. retirees before the crisis in 2008. Retirees were expected to become increasingly responsible for saving for retirement and manage the concomitant risks on their own. This increased nancial risk exposure of individuals should contribute to higher wealth levels in order to compensate for the greater nancial risks. Retirees who were able to rely less on traditional pensions and Social Security to cover their basic expenses indeed accumulated more wealth than those who could not, but not enough to generate the same level of retirement income

TABLE 4 Regression Estimates for Market Risk and Marketable Wealth for Retirees, 1989 to 2007

Explanatory variables	Wealth to income	Potential income minus annuity income to discretionary income, with longevity risk exposure	Potential income minus annuity income to discretionary income, with market risk exposure	Potential income minus annuity income to discretionary income, with market and longevity risk exposure	Equity out of financial assets	Houses out of total assets
Real income (natural logarithm)	—	—	—	—	0.108***	-0.124***
					(0.020)	(0.009)
Black	-2.215***	-0.056*	-0.275***	-0.117***	0.020	0.133***
	(0.768)	(0.032)	(0.051)	(0.036)	(0.067)	(0.030)
Hispanic	-3.122***	-0.017	-0.182	-0.070	-0.099	0.073
	(0.778)	(0.065)	(0.114)	(0.072)	(0.120)	(0.047)
Other race	-1.114	0.059	0.045	0.136	-0.180	0.029
	(3.333)	(3.316)	(3.318)	(3.317)	(3.317)	(3.316)
Less than high school	-4.266***	-0.008	-0.285***	-0.120***	-0.219***	0.090***
	(0.633)	(0.032)	(0.069)	(0.040)	(0.041)	(0.021)
High school	-2.707***	0.015	-0.106*	-0.071**	-0.182***	0.041**
	(0.595)	(0.027)	(0.057)	(0.036)	(0.031)	(0.017)
Some college	-1.825**	0.030	-0.051	-0.035	-0.089**	0.020
	(0.683)	(0.033)	(0.074)	(0.043)	(0.036)	(0.020)
Single women	-0.622	-0.069*	-0.188**	-0.092**	-0.029	0.021
	(0.662)	(0.038)	(0.082)	(0.045)	(0.048)	(0.027)
Married	-0.370	-0.126***	-0.109	-0.113**	-0.003	0.078***
	(0.620)	(0.037)	(0.082)	(0.045)	(0.044)	(0.023)
Age	-0.309	0.094***	-0.006	0.109***	0.027	-0.019
	(0.336)	(0.018)	(0.043)	(0.023)	(0.023)	(0.014)
Age^2	-0.002	-0.001***	0.0003	-0.001***	-0.0002	0.0001
	(0.002)	(0.0001)	(0.0003)	(0.0001)	(0.0002)	(0.0001)
Risk attitude	-1.528***	0.009	-0.142***	-0.093***	-0.222***	0.060***
	(0.342)	(0.016)	(0.036)	(0.023)	(0.020)	(0.011)

	(1)	(2)	(3)	(4)	(5)	(6)
Home ownership		0.454*** (0.045)	−0.033 (0.112)	0.358*** (0.066)		−0.036 (0.027)
Has annuity income	−3.191*** (0.468)	0.211*** (0.025)	0.403 (0.057)	0.254*** (0.033)		0.031** (0.014)
above twice the poverty line						
1992	1.348 (0.675)	−0.039 (0.041)	−0.137* (0.072)	−0.038 (0.045)	0.072 (0.053)	0.040 (0.026)
1995	0.619 (0.656)	−0.059 (0.040)	−0.105 (0.075)	−0.015 (0.047)	0.091 (0.053)	0.011 (0.026)
1998	0.967* (0.556)	−0.062 (0.043)	0.053 (0.088)	0.068 (0.053)	0.132** (0.053)	0.011 (0.045)
2001	2.013*** (0.525)	−0.039 (0.041)	0.031 (0.083)	0.075 (0.051)	0.172*** (0.052)	0.045* (0.027)
2004	2.296*** (0.787)	−0.088** (0.039)	−0.068 (0.083)	−0.036 (0.046)	0.123** (0.050)	0.096*** (0.027)
2007	2.977*** (0.672)	−0.119*** (0.037)	−0.068 (0.073)	−0.064 (0.041)	0.157*** (0.051)	0.106*** (0.026)
Constant	2.866 (12.217)	−3.149*** (0.641)	0.846 (1.527)	−3.109*** (0.850)	−1.244 (0.883)	2.225*** (0.509)
N	3,497	3,497	3,497	3,497	3,497	3,497
F statistics	103.16***				3,497	3,497
Adjusted R^2	0.095	0.104	0.137	0.099	0.182	0.349

Note. Risk regressions are censored regressions. All demographic variables refer to the head of household. Risk attitude measures a household's willingness to take financial risks on a 4-point scale where a lower number indicates a greater willingness to take financial risks. Regression results derive from a population-weighted regression. The results are robust for unweighted regressions. Missing reference variables are "White," "college," "single men," "renter," and "1989." Author's calculations based on BOG (2009a).

*Indicates significance at the 1% level; **indicates significance at the 5% level; and ***indicates significance at the 10% level.

security and protection from nancial market risks. Put differently, the basic income security of America's retirees was already declining before the crisis, as traditional pensions became less prevalent, Social Security bene ts were gradually reduced, and nancial risks associated with private savings remained high.

My results lead to three policy conclusions. First, public policy should help to reduce the risk exposure of retirees. My research indicates that greater annuitization of nancial wealth can make a substantial difference in retirement income security by eliminating longevity risk. Second, policy makers should support efforts of families to save more in order to build more of a cushion for the eventuality that nancial risks materialize as they did in 2007 and thereafter. My results indicate that retirees with lower annuities from Social Security and pensions did not compensate for this lack of income security by suf ciently saving to compensate for their market risk exposure. Third, policy makers should maintain and strengthen retirement savings vehicles that offer lifetime annuities to retirees, where feasible. My results show that so far retirees have not saved enough and have not suf - ciently reduced nancial risks to compensate for the greater individual risk exposure in private retirement savings.

The nancial and economic crisis after 2007 exacerbated trends that had existed for decades because nancial risks materialized after retirees had already become increasingly exposed to such risks. Policy makers should focus on improving the balance between personal responsibility and secured and guaranteed sources of retirement income.

NOTES

[1]The differences are robust with averages, with all non-retirement wealth, and with non-housing wealth.

[2]My analysis sets earnings and personal saving to zero, which is common to retirement income adequacy studies.

[3]See Garner and Verbrugge (2007) for a discussion of the relevant literature, the methodology, and the data.

[4]I assume that annuities and transfer payments will grow with in ation.

[5]This conclusion also holds when total risk-adjusted potential income is related to permanent income.

[6]The results are robust when I use non-housing wealth to income as the dependent variable.

REFERENCES

Benartzi, S., & Thaler, R. (2007). Heuristics and biases in retirement savings behavior. *Journal of Economic Perspectives, 21*(3), 81–104.

Bernheim, D. B. (1997). The adequacy of personal retirement saving: Issues and options In D. A. Wise (Ed.), *Facing the age wave.* Stanford, CA: Hoover Institute Press.

(BOG) Board of Governors, Federal Reserve System. (2009a). *Survey of Consumer Finances, various years*. Washington, DC: BOG.

(BOG) Board of Governors, Federal Reserve System. (2009b). *Release H.15: Selected interest rates*. Washington, DC: BOG.

Browning, M., & Lusardi, A., (1996). Household saving: Micro theories and macro facts. *Journal of Economic Literature, 34*, 1797–1855.

(BLS) Bureau of Labor Statistics. (2008). *National Compensation Survey*. Washington, DC: BLS.

(BLS) Bureau of Labor Statistics. (2009). *Updated CPI-U-RS, all items and all items less food and energy, 1978–2008*. Washington, DC: BLS.

Butrica, B., Murphy, D., & Zedlewski, S. R. (2007). *How many struggle to get by in retirement? CRR working paper No. 2007-27*. Boston, MA: Center for Retirement Research at Boston College.

Carroll, C., & Samwick, A. (1998). How important is precautionary saving? *Review of Economics and Statistics, 80*, 410–419.

(CRR) Center for Retirement Research. (2006). *Retirements at risk: A new national retirement risk index*. Boston, MA: Center for Retirement Research at Boston College.

Copeland, C. (2006). Debt of the elderly and near elderly, 1992–2004. *EBRI Notes, 27*(9), 2–13, Washington, DC: Employee Bene t Research Institute.

Copeland, C. (2007). *How are new retirees doing financially in retirement? EBRI Issue Brief No. 302*. Washington, DC: Employee Bene t Research Institute.

(EBSA) Employee Bene t Security Administration. (2008). *Private pension bulletin 2006, Abstract Form 5500*. Washington, DC: EBSA.

Engen, E. M., & Gale, W. G. (2000). *The effects of 401(k) plans on household wealth: Differences across earnings groups*. Washington, DC: The Brookings Institution.

Engen, E. M., Gale, W. G., & Uccello, C. E. (1999). The adequacy of household saving. *Brookings Papers on Economic Activity, 2*, 65–165.

Englehart, G. (1999). *Have 401(k)s raised household saving? Evidence from the Health and Retirement Study, Aging Studies Program. Working Paper No. 14*. Syracuse, NY: Syracuse University.

Fidelity Investments. (2009). *Fidelity reports on 2008 trends in 401(k) plans*. Boston, MA: Fidelity Investments.

Garner, T. I., & Verbrugge, R. (2007). *The puzzling divergence of U.S. rents and user costs, 1980–2004: Summary and extensions. BLS Working Paper No. 409*. Washington, DC: Bureau of Labor Statistics.

Gustman, A., & Steinmeier, T. L. (1999). Effects of pensions on savings: Analysis with data from the health and retirement study. *Carnegie-Rochester Conference Series on Public Policy, 50*(99), 271–324.

Haveman, R., Holden, K., Wolfe, B., Romanov, A. (2005). *Assessing the maintenance of savings sufficiency over the first decade of retirement. CESIfo Working Paper No. 1567*. Munich, Germany: CESIfo.

Henle, P. (1972). Recent trends in retirement bene ts related to earnings. *Monthly Labor Review, 95*(6), 12–20.

Holden, S., VanDerhei, J., Alonso, L., & Copeland, C. (2008). 401(k) plan asset allocation, account balances, and loan activity in 2007. *Research Perspective, 14*(3), Washington, DC: Investment Company Institute.

Holst, R. (2005). *Wealth accumulation with risky social security: empirical evidence from US micro and macro data.* Unpublished manuscript. Chicago, IL: University of Chicago.

Huberman, G., & Jiang, W. (2006). Offering versus choice in 401(K) plans: Equity exposure and number of funds. *Journal of Finance, 61*(2), 763–801.

Hurd, M., & Panis, C. (2006). The choice to cash out pension rights at job change or retirement. *Journal of Public Economics, 90*(12), 2213–2227.

Iyengar, S., & Kamenica, E. (2006). *Choice overload and simplicity seeking. Working paper.* New York: Columbia University.

Love, D., Smith, P., & McNair, L. (2007). *Do households have enough wealth for retirement? Finance and Economics Discussion Series, No. 2007-17.* Washington, DC: Board of Governors, Federal Reserve System.

Love, D., Smith, P., & McNair, L. (2008). A new look at the wealth adequacy of older U.S. households. *Review of Income and Wealth, 54*(4), 616–642.

Mitchell, O., Mottola, G. R., & Utkus, S. (2005). *The inattentive participant: Portfolio trading behavior in 401(k) behavior. Pension Research Council Working Paper 2006-5.* Philadelphia, PA: Pension Research Council, Wharton School, University of Pennsylvania.

Mitchell, O., & Utkus, S. (2004). *Pension design and structure: New lessons from behavioral finance.* New York, NY: Oxford University Press.

Moore, J. F., & Mitchell, O. S. (2000). Projected retirement wealth and saving adequacy. In O. Mitchell, B. Hammond, & A. Rappaport (Eds.), *Forecasting retirement needs and retirement wealth.* Philadelphia, PA: University of Pennsylvania Press.

Munnell, A., Golub-Sass, F., Soto, M., & Vitagliano, F. (2006). *Why are healthy employers freezing their pension plans? Issue in Brief No. 44.* Boston, MA: Center for Retirement Research at Boston College.

Munnell, A., Golub-Sass, F., & Webb, A. (2007). *What moves the National Retirement Risk Index? A look back and an update. Issue in Brief No. 7-1.* Boston, MA: Center for Retirement Research at Boston College.

Munnell, A., & Soto, M. (2005). *How do pensions affect replacement rates? Issue in Brief No. 37.* Boston, MA: Center for Retirement Research at Boston College.

Munnell, A. & Sunden, A. (2004) *Coming up short: The challenge of 401(k) plans.* Washington, DC: Brookings Institution Press.

(OFHEO) Of ce of Federal Housing Enterprise Oversight. (2009). *Home Price Index.* Washington, DC: OFHEO.

Papke, L. (1999). Are 401(k) plans replacing other employer-provided pensions? Evidence from panel data. *Journal of Human Resources, 34*(2), 46–68.

Perun, P. (2007). Putting annuities back into savings plans. In T. Ghilarducci & C. Weller (Eds), *Employee pensions: Policies, problems, and possibilities.* Champaign IL: Labor and Employment Relations Association.

Poterba, J., Rauh, J., Venti, S., & Wise, A. (2007). De ned contribution plans, de ned bene t plans, and the accumulation of retirement wealth. *Journal of Public Economics, 91*(10), 2062–2086.

Poterba, J., Venti, S., & Wise, A. (2007). *The changing landscape of pensions in the United States. NBER Working Paper No. 13381.* Cambridge, MA: National Bureau of Economic Research.

Reid, B., & Holden, S. (2008). *Retirement saving in wake of financial market volatility*. Washington, DC: Investment Company Institute.

RETIRE Project. (2001). *2001 RETIRE project report*. Atlanta, GA: Georgia State University.

Russell, L. H., Bruce, E. A., & Conahan, J. (2006). *A methodology to determine economic security for elders*. Boston, MA: Gerontology Institute, University of Massachusetts Boston, and Washington, DC: Wider Opportunities for Women.

VanDerhei, J., Holden, S., Alonso, L., & Copeland, C. (2008). *401(k) plan asset allocation, account balances, and loan activity in 2007. EBRI Issue Brief No. 324*. Washington, DC: Employee Bene t Research Institute.

Weller, C. (2009). *Risk matters: Retirees exposed to growing risks*. Paper presented at the "Financial Institutions and Economic Security" conference of the Innovation Knowledge Development network and The Open University, London, UK, May 21.

Weller, C., & Sabatini, K. (2008). From boom to bust: Did the nancial fragility of homeowners increase in an era of greater nancial deregulation? *Journal of Economic Issues, 42*(3), 607–632.

Weller, C., & Wolff, E. (2005). *Retirement security: The particular role of social security*. Washington, DC: Economic Policy Institute.

Early Retiree and Near-Elderly Health Insurance in Recession

ELISE GOULD, PhD

Director, Health Policy Research, Economic Policy Institute, Washington, DC, USA

ALEXANDER HERTEL-FERNANDEZ, BA

Research Assistant, Economic Policy Institute, Washington, DC, USA

This paper examines recent trends in health insurance cost and coverage for the near-elderly population (aged 55 to 64), with particular attention directed toward the implications of the 2007 recession. We examine coverage by demographic and socioeconomic characteristics from the Current Population Survey and the Medical Expenditure Panel Survey. We also estimate the effects of projected increases in the unemployment rate for employer-sponsored insurance coverage of the near elderly in 2009 and 2010. Erosion in coverage is likely to be exacerbated in the short run by the 2007 recession, given rapidly rising unemployment among this age cohort, and in the long-run, given the inability of the labor market to support increased labor market participation of older Americans in jobs that would have traditionally provided health insurance coverage.

INTRODUCTION

The economic downturn that began in 2007 has cast the erosion of health insurance for the near-elderly population (aged 55 to 64) in stark light, as headlines ll with stories of employers terminating or retrenching retiree bene ts. Although, on average, Americans aged 55 to 64 still have lower rates of "uninsurance" than the general population, the near elderly have a greater need for health care and, in turn, affordable health insurance coverage, making the effects of uninsurance all the more detrimental. Furthermore, there are disparities in insurance coverage within the near-elderly population, with poorer and less healthy individuals more likely to go without coverage. This paper extends and updates previous research on trends in the cost and coverage of health insurance for the near-elderly population, with particular focus on the effects of the economic recession from 2007 to 2009 using recently released data for 2008.

We document low coverage for the near-elderly population, especially for minority, poorly educated, and less healthy individuals, in tandem with a decline in the number of rms offering coverage to early retirees. The recession has begun to take a toll on the already vulnerable near elderly. Using data from the 2009 March Supplement to the Current Population Survey (CPS), we nd a decline in employer-sponsored insurance coverage between 2007 and 2008 of 1 percentage point (or 650,000 individuals) and a corresponding rise in the rates of public coverage (0.2 percentage points, or 250,000 individuals) and in the uninsured (0.5 percentage points, or 290,000 individuals).

We estimate that rising unemployment since 2008 will result in a loss of employer-sponsored health insurance for approximately one million near-elderly individuals in 2009 and about another 200,000 in 2010. Based on the past and projected erosion of near-elderly health insurance, particularly for retirees, we conclude that there is a strong case for substantial health reform that addresses the needs of the near-elderly population.

We rst review the body of research on health insurance coverage for the near elderly and highlight its importance for health status and the decision to retire. Next, we characterize trends in health and health insurance coverage for the near-elderly population using data from the CPS. We then examine rm-level trends in the offering of retiree insurance and trends in the cost of coverage from the Medical Expenditure Panel Survey's Insurance Component (MEPS-IC). In the fourth section, we discuss the effect of a worsening labor market and decline of household wealth on health insurance coverage. Given that the available data only capture the beginning of the recession's effect through 2008, we make projections to examine the magnitude of anticipated increases in unemployment rate on employer-sponsored insurance (ESI) in 2009 and 2010. We conclude by summarizing our ndings, outlining the need for comprehensive national health reform, and brie y reviewing a more modest policy option—early Medicare buy-in—for covering the near elderly within broader health reform.

LITERATURE REVIEW

Prior work has characterized the near-elderly population and its unique need for continuous, affordable health insurance coverage. Incidences of disability and chronic illness are all higher for the near-elderly population and continue to rise with age (Gruber & Madrian, 1996; Nichols, 2001). Rates of disease and chronic conditions among 55- to 64-year-olds are also heavily stratified by socioeconomic characteristics, with incidence of high blood pressure, heart disease, cancer, diabetes, and arthritis steadily increasing as household income and educational attainment fall (Collins, Davis, Shoen, Doty, & Kriss, 2008).

Although average levels of coverage are higher than in the general population, Swartz and Stevenson (2001) provide the important distinction between two groups within the near-elderly cohort. The first group is better educated, healthier, higher-income, and more likely to have health insurance, while the second group is poorer, less educated, and sicker. Holahan (2004) reexamines these divisions and finds evidence that the poor and less healthy near elderly still suffer from alarmingly high rates of uninsurance. This is particularly true for the near elderly still in the workforce; non-retirees had an uninsurance rate of 35% in 2002 compared to a 17% rate for their retired counterparts (Holahan, 2004).

For the near elderly, a lack of insurance is much more detrimental to health status than for other adults (Vistnes, Cooper, Bernard, & Banthin, 2009). The importance of coverage for health outcomes is borne out by the expenditures of near-elderly individuals who were previously uninsured before enrolling in Medicare. Though the estimated magnitude of health improvement upon receiving Medicare coverage varies from considerable (see for example McWilliams, Meara, Zaslavsky, & Ayanian, 2009; Hadley & Waidmann, 2006; Dor, Sudano, & Baker, 2006) to small (see for example Polsky et al., 2009), there is a consensus that being previously uninsured after age 50 raises Medicare spending and the expected risk of mortality (Baker et al., 2006). Relative to their need, the near elderly have a much more challenging time than other age groups obtaining affordable coverage. Although they are second to children in access to public insurance, for many without ESI, the individual market is typically the only alternative. Given that individual plans are priced according to expected risk, the near elderly are frequently charged much higher premiums. Furthermore, the limited protection offered by individual insurance, as well as the risk of rescission, places the near elderly at a much greater likelihood for financial distress should they require extensive medical care (Pollitz & Sorian, 2002; Harbage & Hayock, 2009).

The near elderly are more likely to begin to leave the labor force than other adults, and health status and health insurance coverage are both important factors in their decisions to retire. There are two central (and overlapping) components of the health and employment dynamic. First, the near elderly are more likely than other adults to report health problems and be forced to leave the labor market due to poor health (Short, Shea, & Powell, 2001). For example, Burtless and Mof tt (1987) nd that 26% of respondents in the 1969–1979 Retirement Health Survey left jobs due to health problems, a conclusion echoed by later research by Packard and Reno (1989), who nd that 24% of newly retired Social Security bene ciaries indicated poor health as their primary reason for leaving the workforce.

Second, having ESI appears to be a strong motivation for the near elderly to stay in the labor force longer than they might if health insurance were not linked to employment. Gruber and Madrian (2002) nd that employer-provided retiree insurance coverage is a clear determinant of the decision to leave the labor force, especially for those who are ineligible for pubic insurance. Other research demonstrates that the likelihood of retiring due to health insurance availability increases as individuals age (Hurd & McGarry, 1996; Rust & Phelan, 1997; Anderson, Gustman, & Steinmeier, 1999; Blau & Gilleskie, 2008). This effect is present in married couples, who have been found to delay "joint" retirement until either partner secured retiree health insurance coverage, typically the wife (Blau & Gilleskie, 2006; Kapur & Rogowski, 2009).

Given the importance of continuous coverage for the near elderly, historical trends in the erosion of ESI are particularly worrisome (Gould, 2008; Weller, Wenger, & Gould, 2004a). The erosion is driven by declining employee take-up and reduced offer rates in smaller rms, which both in turn are linked to rapid increases in health insurance costs (Shen & Long, 2006; Cutler, 2002). Health insurance premiums have grown a cumulative 131% between 1999 and 2008, outpacing wage growth of 33% over the same period (Kaiser/Health Research & Educational Trust, 2008). Furthermore, ESI for retirees—the principal source of coverage for early retirees who do not yet qualify for Medicare—is also in decline (Weller, Wenger, & Gould, 2004b). Recent research has found that only about one-quarter of private sector employees worked at rms offering retiree health coverage in 2003, down from 66% in 1988 (Buchmueller, Johnson, & LoSasso, 2006). In response to rapidly rising premiums, employers have recently begun to increase retiree contributions to insurance coverage for those fortunate enough to still receive coverage through their employer. Buchmueller et al. (2006) also nd that more than a third of rms offering coverage increased the cost-sharing responsibility of retired workers.

DATA

Our analysis makes use of three data sources: the CPS March Supplement, the MEPS-IC, and the monthly CPS.

We use the CPS March Supplement, a nationally representative survey of approximately 78,000 households conducted by the Census Bureau, to measure health and health insurance coverage by various demographic and socioeconomic characteristics among the near-elderly population from 2000 to 2008. Health insurance in the CPS March Supplement is measured by asking the interviewee whether he or she had different forms of coverage at any given point during the year. Given the format of the question, it is possible for an individual to be coded with multiple forms of coverage within a single year. Therefore, these rates combined with the uninsured do not sum to 100%.

We also use publically available data from the MEPS-IC to look at the number and types of rms offering health insurance to workers and retirees from 1997 to 2008. The MEPS-IC conducts annual, nationally representative surveys of more than 35,000 private-sector establishments. Finally, we use the Bureau of Labor Statistics' monthly unemployment rate for the 55 to 64 population, calculated from the monthly CPS for 2000 to 2009.

HEALTH AND HEALTH INSURANCE FOR THE NEAR ELDERLY

In 2008, 55- to 64-year-olds had the second-highest rates of ESI coverage through their own jobs, second only to prime working-age adults, those aged 45 to 54 years (Table 1). Nearly three-fourths of the near elderly with ESI receive coverage through their own employers, with the remaining share covered as dependents (such as a spouse or partner). Combined, ESI coverage for the near elderly falls to third-highest among the age groups.

The near elderly have the highest rate of non-group, direct-purchase insurance (9.8%) and a rate of public insurance (20.1%) rivaled only by children, many of whom have access to Medicaid through the Children's Health Insurance Program. The disproportionate share of the near elderly with non-group insurance is of concern, given the often inadequate protection offered by these policies and the greater health needs of the near-elderly population.

TABLE 1 Source of Health Insurance Coverage by Age, 2008

Age	ESI-own	ESI-dependent	Non-group	Public	Uninsured
0–18	0.4%	58.2%	5.1%	32.7%	10.3%
19–34	36.5%	17.8%	5.7%	13.7%	28.0%
35–44	47.9%	19.6%	5.9%	11.3%	19.4%
45–54	50.8%	18.8%	7.2%	13.1%	15.9%
55–64	49.5%	17.3%	9.8%	20.1%	12.5%

Note. Source: Authors' analysis of March CPS 2009 data. Shares do not sum to 100% because a nontrivial portion of the population reports having multiple forms of coverage in the same year.

TABLE 2 Source of Insurance Coverage for the Near Elderly by Characteristic, 2008

	ESI	Non-group	Public	Uninsured
All	66.8%	9.8%	20.1%	12.5%
Race and ethnicity				
White	68.5%	10.2%	18.9%	11.7%
Black	57.9%	6.0%	31.6%	14.9%
Asian	58.9%	11.0%	15.8%	20.8%
Other	56.2%	7.0%	24.0%	20.2%
Hispanic	48.7%	4.6%	22.3%	29.4%
Not Hispanic	68.5%	10.2%	19.9%	10.9%
Education				
Less than high school	36.2%	6.3%	38.9%	26.5%
High school	63.3%	9.1%	22.4%	14.6%
Some college	70.0%	9.7%	19.9%	10.7%
College	77.0%	11.4%	12.0%	8.2%
Advanced degree	79.9%	12.1%	11.0%	5.8%
Self-reported health status				
Excellent	77.2%	12.6%	7.5%	8.8%
Very good	77.5%	9.7%	10.2%	9.6%
Good	67.1%	9.5%	16.7%	15.7%
Fair	47.7%	8.3%	43.1%	16.3%
Poor	30.1%	6.3%	65.5%	13.8%

Note. Source: Authors' analysis of March CPS 2009 data. Shares do not sum to 100% because a nontrivial portion of the population reports having multiple forms of coverage in the same year.

Table 2 examines the sources of coverage for the near-elderly population by demographic and socioeconomic characteristics. In 2008, near-elderly Whites were more likely to have ESI than any other racial or ethnic group (at 68.5%), and Hispanics were the least likely (at 48.7%). Hispanics also had the highest rate of uninsurance, with nearly one-third lacking health insurance of any kind. Coverage is widely strati ed by education. ESI coverage among those without high school diplomas is less than half that of those with college degrees. While rates of public coverage are high for those with less than or a completed high school education (38.9% and 22.4%, respectively), high uninsurance rates still persist among those with low levels of education; 26.5% of those without high school degrees and 14.6% of those with high school diplomas are without any sort of coverage.

There is considerable variation in insurance coverage by self-reported health status. ESI coverage is two and a half times greater among those in excellent or very good health versus those in poor health; the rates exceed 77% for both excellent and very good as opposed to only 30.1% for those in poor health. Rates of non-group, direct-purchase health insurance are also correlated with health status. Coverage is twice as high for those in excellent health compared to poor health (6.3% versus 12.6%), re ecting the dif culty of anyone in less than excellent health in obtaining affordable private insurance with adequate nancial protection. Public health insurance

TABLE 3 Self-Reported Health Status and Ratio of Household Income to the Federal Poverty Line for 55- to 64-Year-Olds, 2008

Self-reported health status	Income-to-poverty line ratio				
	Below 100%	200%	300%	400%	500% or more
Excellent	8.4%	10.2%	13.8%	13.4%	18.5%
Very good	16.3%	18.9%	25.9%	30.5%	34.3%
Good	29.7%	32.1%	32.9%	35.0%	31.6%
Fair	25.5%	23.9%	17.8%	15.3%	11.6%
Poor	20.1%	14.9%	9.6%	5.8%	4.0%
	100%	100%	100%	100%	100%

Note. Source: Authors' analysis of March CPS 2009 data. Income-to-poverty ratio based on Census de ni-tion of income and the poverty threshold, rather than the poverty guidelines. Federal Poverty Threshold was $22,050 for a family of four in 2008.

(largely Medicare and Medicaid), on the other hand, is strongly inversely correlated with health status, with the likelihood of coverage decreasing as health improves. While public insurance covers many in poor health, it does not reach all, and rates of uninsurance are still much greater for those in poor health.

The association between self-reported health status and insurance cov-erage is in part the result of a strong correlation between self-reported health and socioeconomic status for the near elderly, as shown in Table 3. Those in worse health are more likely to be poorer; for example, more than half of all individuals with household incomes 500% or more of the poverty line report being in excellent or good health, while less than one-quarter of those under the poverty line report similar health status.

RETIREE HEALTH INSURANCE

Employer-sponsored health insurance is an essential source of coverage not just for active workers and their dependents but also for retired individuals and their families. Figure 1 documents the erosion of retiree health insurance for the near elderly from 1997 to 2008. During this period, the number of private-sector rms offering insurance for retirees younger than 65 was nearly cut in half, from 21.6% to 11.2%. Insurance plan offers for retirees older than 65 followed a similar trend (not shown), declining from 19.5% in 2000 to 10.5% in 2008. In terms of overall trends, the number of rms offering any sort of health insurance to their workers has increased slightly since 2000.

Patterns of retiree and early retiree health insurance coverage vary widely across rm characteristics but generally mirror those of general health insurance offering, albeit at much lower levels. As shown in Table 4, early

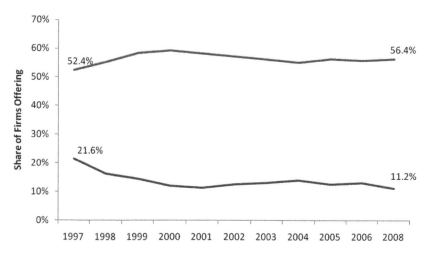

FIGURE 1 Trends in the share of rms offering insurance, 1997–2008.

Source: authors' analysis of 1997–2008 MEPS data.

TABLE 4 Percentage of Private-Sector Firms Offering Health Insurance and Retiree Health Insurance, 2008

	Offering health insurance	Offering retiree health insurance to those younger than 65	Offering health insurance to those older than 65
All firms	56.4%	11.2%	10.5%
Firm size			
<10 employees	35.6%	1.4%	2.3%
10–24 employees	66.1%	1.6%	3.4%
25–99 employees	81.3%	2.4%	2.9%
100–999 employees	95.4%	8.0%	7.7%
1,000+ employees	98.9%	36.1%	31.1%
Industry			
Agriculture, sh, forestry	28.6%	2.4%	3.0%
Mining and manufacturing	69.7%	7.2%	7.2%
Construction	42.3%	3.2%	3.3%
Utilities and transportation	58.6%	23.7%	21.3%
Wholesale trade	68.2%	9.5%	9.4%
Financial services and real estate	66.3%	26.2%	22.7%
Retail trade	60.1%	15.9%	12.9%
Professional services	61.1%	6.8%	7.2%
Other services	47.8%	6.2%	7.2%

Note. Source: Authors' analysis of 2008 MEPS data.

retiree coverage is extremely low in small to medium-sized businesses, reaching 8.0% for rms with 100 to 999 workers. For large rms with 1,000 or more employees, coverage is much higher, at 36.1%. Near-elderly coverage is heavily concentrated among a handful of industries: only three industries have rates above 10% and only two—utilities/transportation and nancial services/real estate—have rates above 20%. As with overall health insurance offering rates, early retiree health insurance coverage is much more likely in rms with higher levels of full-time workers and a union presence (data not shown).

Early retirees fortunate enough to receive health insurance coverage from their employers must also grapple with rapidly rising premium levels. From 2000 to 2003, average premiums for single and family early retiree health insurance policies rose by 44% and 35%, respectively (*Mercer Retiree Health Benefits Survey*, 2007; Zawacki, 2006). In light of these increases, many employers have begun to shift more of the nancial responsibility of coverage to workers and limiting eligibility for new hires. According to a representative industry survey, at least 10% of large employers (1,000 or more workers) have been increasing the share of health policy premiums that retirees must pay out of pocket for the past 5 years (*Kaiser/Hewitt Survey on Retiree Health Benefits*, 2006). Indeed, the same survey found that just over half of all large rms required the entire premium to be paid by retirees.

EFFECTS OF THE 2007 RECESSION ON INSURANCE COVERAGE

The recession that began in 2007 has taken a heavy toll on the entire workforce and by nearly all measures is the longest and deepest economic downturn since the Great Depression. The economy has shed more jobs more rapidly than in any other recession in the postwar era, creating serious problems for health insurance coverage. Increased unemployment generally leads to more workers losing their ESI, forcing them into the individual insurance market or to go without any coverage. This is particularly disruptive to the near-elderly population, given their increased need for medical services and for continuity in health care providers. Research has consistently shown that becoming uninsured for even short periods of time can cause individuals to delay or forgo needed medical care, resulting in poorer health and greater out-of-pocket medical expenses when the individual becomes insured again (Schoen & DesRoches, 2000; Sudano & Baker, 2003).

The near-elderly population generally fares the best out of any other age group during economic downturns, given generally higher tenure and employment experience. Furthermore, an increasing number of the near elderly have been joining the labor force, indicating a response to rising costs of living, particularly in health care (Garr, 2009). Until the 2007 recession, the greatest percentage point change and highest rate of near-elderly unemployment throughout the past three business cycles occurred during the 1981–1982 recession, when the rate rose from 3.4% to 6.8%, a change of 3.4 percentage points. Since December 2007, the rate has increased by

3.9 percentage points, from 3.0% to 6.9% in August 2009—worse than all three past recessions.

These dramatic increases in near-elderly unemployment drive corresponding losses in ESI coverage. The rate of ESI coverage declined by 1.0 percentage point (650,000 individuals) from 2007 to 2008 to a rate of 66.8% in 2008. While there was a corresponding increase in the rate of public coverage by 0.2 percentage points (250,000 individuals), to 20.1%, this was insuf cient to capture all of those without workplace coverage. The rate of the uninsured grew by 0.5 percentage points (290,000 individuals), to 12.5%.

The labor market continued to deteriorate into 2009 and is expected to worsen in 2010. Both the Congressional Budget Of ce and the Of ce of Management and Budget, in their 2009 mid-session budget reviews, predicted that the average unemployment would continue to rise through 2010 (CBO, 2009; OMB, 2009). Using a historical ratio of the 55 to 64 unemployment rate to the overall unemployment (compiled from Bureau of Labor Statistics historical data), we project the near-elderly unemployment rates for a national unemployment rate of 9.3 and 10.2, as has been estimated for 2009 and 2010,[1] respectively. Given this prediction of the overall unemployment rate, Americans aged 55 to 64 could experience an annual unemployment rate of 6.7% and 7.3%, respectively, for the same period. These rates are likely to be much worse for demographic subsets of the population, particularly for minorities and males. Though certainly imprecise, this calculation provides a rough estimate of the expected effect the continuing recession will have for the near-elderly population.

Previous econometric research has attempted to isolate and estimate the effects of changes in the unemployment rate on health insurance coverage (see for example Cawley & Simon, 2005; Holahan & Bowen Garrett, 2009). These studies have found that a one percentage point increase in the unemployment rate is associated with a 0.91 to 1.01 percentage point decline in ESI coverage of nonelderly adults. While the coef cients from the literature were not directly estimated on the near-elderly population, we use them to calculate present and projected effects of the 2007 recession on trends in health insurance for the near elderly.[2] Although the coef cients we apply are for the overall younger-than-65 population, we believe that our estimates are sound and, if anything, offer a lower bound on ESI losses for this subpopulation because they have higher rates of coverage and lower rates of unemployment at the start of the recession.

We estimate that a 3 percentage point rise in unemployment for the 55 to 64 population in 2009 will lower ESI coverage by 2.7 to 3.0 percentage points, or by approximately 926,000, to 1.04 million individuals. Note that this calculation measures the effect of unemployment on health insurance coverage in isolation, independent of other effects that may change the overall trend in coverage in either direction. If the near-elderly unemployment rate rises to 7.3%, as is predicted for 2010, we estimate that ESI will lower by 3.2 to 3.6 percentage points, or by 1.11 to 1.25 million individuals.

The effects of the 2007 recession are not limited to those who lose or lack coverage. Household wealth 1 year after the start of the recession (the most recent data) has fallen by $15 trillion, the greatest decline in over 50 years, leaving individuals and families far more exposed to shocks in income and expenditures (Flow of Funds Accounts of the United States, 2008). This has important implications for the growing number of individuals without adequate health insurance coverage—the so-called underinsured. Approximately 25 million nonelderly adults have policies that do not provide suf cient nancial protection, leaving them to pay 10% or more of medical expenses out-of-pocket (Schoen, Collins, Kriss, & Doty, 2008). Indeed, recent research has shown that household assets appear to be a far more important determinant of adequate health insurance coverage than income (Bernard, Banthin, & Encinosa, 2009).

Given that during past periods of economic hardship employers have scaled back their obligations to retirees (Jones, 2008), either by cutting retiree insurance coverage or by increasing cost-sharing, it is likely that nancial protection against health costs will continue to diminish for the near elderly, exposing them to increased risk just as many have lost assets in the economic downturn. The Commonwealth Fund found that 53% of employers reported that they would increase their workers' contributions to retiree health premiums from 2007 to 2009 and 43% will increase the amount retirees must pay out-of-pocket for prescription drugs during the same period (*The Commonwealth Fund/National Opinion Research Center Survey of Retiree Health Benefits*, 2007). The same survey found that 20% of rms were planning to discontinue existing retirees' health coverage and that 19% plan to discontinue retiree bene ts for future employees. In light of the worsening economy, these trends will likely accelerate. It is likely that retiree health insurance will represent a smaller and smaller factor in overall coverage rates for the near elderly in the future without public intervention that requires employers to continue coverage or that provides for some public reinsurance fund in case rms no longer can afford to provide bene ts.

Although disaggregated data for the nonelderly are not available, it is reasonable to assume that underinsurance is comparatively riskier for the near elderly relative to other demographic groups, given their increased potential for chronic diseases and intensive medical procedures. This is particularly true for the nearly 10% of 55- to 64-year-olds with individual, direct-purchase health insurance, which has been shown to provide far less nancial protection than group policies through higher deductibles, higher patient co-payments, and fewer covered bene ts (Gabel, Dhont, Whitmore, & Pickreign, 2002). However, even for retirees with ESI, health insurance can be a considerable drain on savings and assets. A 65-year-old couple with average life expectancy and health needs would need up to $361,000 to cover premiums and out-of-pocket costs for their employer-sponsored plans throughout the rest of their lives starting in 2009 (Fronstin, 2006, adjusted for medical in ation).

DISCUSSION

This paper updates trends in health insurance cost and coverage for the near elderly, highlighting the overall erosion in coverage rates and incidence of rm offering. We also nd disparities in coverage by health, demographic, and socioeconomic characteristics: less educated, poorer, and sicker near-elderly adults are more likely to lack employer-sponsored health insurance. The 2007 recession and rising unemployment rate will likely exacerbate these trends.

The American Recovery and Reinvestment Act of 2009 took steps to help households maintain health insurance coverage by expanding the COBRA program, which permits eligible involuntarily terminated employees and their families to keep their employer-sponsored health insurance. Before the act was passed, the terminated employee was required to pay the entire cost of the insurance plan on their own, without employer contributions. For the average household, the full cost of an ESI plan could consume 84% of their unemployment bene ts (*Paychecks or premiums*, 2009). The act provides a 65% reduction in the premiums of workers involuntarily terminated between September and December 2009, thereby making COBRA much more affordable for eligible workers. That said, COBRA fails to reach signi cant portions of the working population, since it only covers workers who were enrolled in health insurance before termination. Moreover, COBRA does not extend to retired workers whose employer decides to eliminate coverage, a nontrivial share of the near-elderly uninsured. Therefore, while COBRA expansions are an important rst step to help the uninsured weather the recession, they must also be coupled with broader coverage expansions to be relevant for near-elderly uninsured and underinsured.

Comprehensive national reform should at least include a new regulated national health insurance exchange for individuals and rms to purchase coverage and a nationally operated public insurance option as part of that marketplace to compete against existing private insurers (see for example Hacker, 2006). The pricing of premiums in the new national exchange calls into question issues of equity between people of different ages. Full community rating of plans would be most bene cial for the near elderly and other high-risk groups but could potentially raise costs for younger and lower-risk enrollees. Some proposals have thus called for permissible variation in plan pricing by age; however, the greater the variation permitted, the less affordable coverage will be for high-risk elderly populations. High premium costs for the young could be partially offset by generous subsidies for enrollees. Viewed from a life-course perspective, community rating proves to be the best method of spreading out the risk of catastrophic medical expenses and medical in ation across one's lifetime and between the young and the old (Jack, 1998; Hertel-Fernandez, 2009).

Policy interventions to improve insurance coverage of the near-elderly population need not rest entirely with comprehensive national health reform; there are speci c proposals that could be implemented in the short term as a precursor to more expansive change. One such proposal is an early Medicare buy-in program for Americans younger than 65 (see for example Johnson, Moon, & Davidoff, 2002 and AARP, 2008). Eligible individuals could pay actuarially adjusted premiums for Medicare services in addition to a small fee for administrative costs. This is not unprecedented, as individuals without suf cient work history but who are older than 65 can buy into Medicare coverage. Aside from covering the uninsured, a Medicare buy-in carries the promise of lowering future Medicare costs by improving the health of the near elderly before they enroll in the traditional program.

Proposals for a Medicare buy-in, however, must adequately address issues of risk pooling, premium design, and enrollment to be successful in reducing the ranks of the near-elderly uninsured. Adverse selection could be reduced by providing premium subsidies (in order to make enrollment more appealing for low-risk individuals) and changing eligibility to include low-risk younger enrollees or limiting enrollment to older enrollees (62 and older) who are more homogenous in health status. Policy makers must also decide whether enrollees who already have insurance would be eligible. Given the inadequacy of individual insurance policies for high-risk groups, such as the near elderly, it may be bene cial to allow private plan holders to switch to Medicare. Most proposals, however, do not permit individuals with ESI to enroll to prevent further erosion of workplace insurance or retiree coverage. An unintended consequence of the program would be the early retirement of some near elderly who were only staying employed to continue receiving insurance coverage. These concerns, in addition to the cost of premium subsidies, must be weighed against the gains in insurance coverage and health status for high-risk near-elderly individuals.

The near-elderly population is uniquely affected by the worsening health insurance system in the United States because they are more likely to experience illnesses and less likely to be able to obtain continuous affordable coverage relative to younger adults. Furthermore, the costs generated by the sick and uninsured near elderly are passed on to Medicare in the form of higher spending when these individuals become eligible for enrollment. Given these important vulnerabilities and disparities, national health reform must take steps speci cally to address the needs of this population.

NOTES

1. See Mishel, Shierholz, and Marcus (2009) for a further discussion of this methodology.
2. Assumes a baseline unemployment rate of 4.6%; see Holahan and Bowen Garrett (2009) for a further discussion.

REFERENCES

AARP. (2008). A Medicare buy-in program. In *Insight on the Issues*. Washington, DC: AARP Public Policy Institute.

Anderson, P. M., Gustman, A. L., & Steinmeier, T. L. (1999). Trends in male labor force participation and retirement: Some evidence on the role of pensions and social security in the 1970s and 1980s. *Journal of Labor Economics, 17*(4), 757–793.

Baker, D., Sudano, J., Durazo-Arvizo, R., Feinglass, J., Witt, W., & Thompson, J. (2006). Health insurance coverage and the risk of decline in overall health and death among the near elderly, 1992–2002. *Medical Care, 44*(3), 277–282.

Bernard, D. M., Banthin, J. S., & Encinosa, W. E. (2009). Wealth, income, and the affordability of health insurance. *Health Affairs, 28*(3), 887–896.

Blau, D., & Gilleskie, D. (2006). Health insurance and retirement of married couples. *Journal of Applied Economics, 21*(7), 935–953.

Blau, D., & Gilleskie, D. (2008). The role of retiree health insurance in the employment behavior of older men. *International Economic Review, 49*(2), 475–514.

Buchmueller, T., Johnson, R. J., & LoSasso, A. T. (2006). Trends in retiree health insurance. *Health Affairs, 25*(6), 1507–1516.

Burtless, G., & Mof tt, R. A. (1987). Occupational effects on the health and work capacity of older men. In G. Burtless (Ed.), *Work, health, and income among the elderly*. Washington, DC: The Brookings Institution.

Cawley, J., & Simon, K. I. (2005). Health insurance coverage and the macroeconomy. *Journal of Health Economics, 24*(2), 299–315.

CBO. (2009). *The budget and economic outlook: An update*. Washington, DC: Author.

Collins, S. R., Davis, K., Schoen, C., Doty, M. M., & Kriss, J. L. (2008). Health coverage for aging baby boomers. In R. W. Eberts & R. A. Hobbie (Eds.), *Older and out of work: Jobs and social insurance for a changing economy*. Kalamazoo, MI: W.E. Upjohn Institute for Employment Research.

The Commonwealth Fund/National Opinion Research Center Survey of Retiree Health Benefits. (2007). New York, NY: The Commonwealth Fund.

Cutler, D. (2002). Employee costs and the decline in health insurance coverage. In *National Bureau of Economic Research Working Papers*. Cambridge, MA: National Bureau of Economic Research.

Dor, A., Sudano, J., & Baker, D. (2006). The effect of private insurance on the health of older, working age adults: Evidence from the Health and Retirement Study. *Health Services Research, 41*(3, pt 1), 759–787.

Flow of Funds Accounts of the United States. (2008). *Federal Reserve statistical review*. Washington, DC: Federal Reserve.

Fronstin, P. (2006). *Savings needed to fund health insurance and health care expenses in retirement*. Washington, DC: Employee Bene t Research Institute Brief.

Gabel, J., Dhont, K., Whitmore, H., & Pickreign, J. (2002). Individual insurance: How much nancial protection does it provide? *Health Affairs*, Web Exclusive.

Garr, E. (2009). *Older Americans in the recession*. Washington, DC: Economic Policy Institute.

Gould, E. (2008). *The erosion of employer-sponsored health insurance. Briefing Paper No. 223*. Washington, DC: Economic Policy Institute.

Gruber, J., & Madrian, B. (1996). Health insurance, labor supply and the retirement decision. *American Economic Review, 85*(4), 938–948.

Gruber, J., & Madrian, B. (2002). *Health insurance, labor supply, and job mobility: A critical review of the literature. Working Paper #8817*. Cambridge, MA: National Bureau of Economic Research.

Hacker, J. (2006). *Health care for America*. Washington, DC: Economic Policy Institute.

Hadley, J., & Waidmann, T. (2006). Health insurance and health at age 65: Implications for medical care spending on new Medicare bene ciaries. *Health Services Research, 41*(2), 429–451.

Harbage, P., & Hayock, H. (2009). *Primer on post-claims underwriting. Policy Brief*. Princeton, NJ: Robert Wood Johnson Foundation.

Hertel-Fernandez, A. (2009). *Whose welfare state? Generational risk sharing in American social policy. Privatization of Risk Working Paper*. Washington, DC: Economic Policy Institute.

Holahan, J. (2004). *Health insurance coverage of the near elderly*. Washington, DC: Kaiser Commission on Medicaid and the Uninsured.

Holahan, J., & Bowen Garrett, A. (2009). *Rising unemployment, Medicaid and the uninsured*. Washington, DC: Kaiser Family Foundation.

Hurd, M. D., & McGarry, K. (1996). *Prospective retirement: Effects of job characteristics, pension, and health insurance*. Los Angeles, CA: University of California at Los Angeles.

Jack, W. G. (1998). Intergenerational risk sharing and health insurance nancing. *The Economic Record, 74*(225), 153–161.

Johnson, R. W., Moon, M., & Davidoff, A., J. (2002). *A Medicare buy-in for the near elderly*. Washington, DC: The Urban Institute.

Jones, C. W. (2008). *Testimony for the hearing on safeguarding retiree health benefits*. Washington, DC: Committee on Education & Labor of the US House of Representatives.

Kaiser/Health Research & Educational Trust. (2008). *Employer health benefits annual survey*. Washington, DC: The Kaiser Family Foundation.

Kaiser/Hewitt Survey on Retiree Health Benefits. (2006). Washington, DC: Kaiser Family Foundation.

Kapur, K., & Rogowski, J. (2009). The role of health insurance in joint retirement among married couples. *Industrial & Labor Relations Review, 60*(3), 397–407.

McWilliams, J. M., Meara, E., Zaslavsky, A. M., & Ayanian J. Z. (2009). Differences in control of cardiovascular disease and diabetes by race, ethnicity, and education: U.S. Trends from 1999 to 2006 and effects of Medicare coverage. *Annals of Internal Medicine, 150*(8), 505–515.

Mercer Retiree Health Benefits Survey. (2007). New York, NY: Mercer Consulting.

Mishel, L., Shierholz, H., & Marcus, T. (2009). *Without adequate public spending, a catastrophic recession for some.* Washington, DC: Economic Policy Institute.

Nichols, L. (2001). Policy options for lling gaps in the health insurance coverage of older workers and early retirees. In P. Budetti, R. Burkhauser, J. Gregory, & H. Hunt (Eds.), *Ensuring health and income security for an aging workforce.* Kalamazoo, MI: W.E. Upjohn Institute for Employment Research.

OMB. (2009). *Mid-session review.* Washington, DC: Of ce of Management and Budget.

Paychecks or premiums. (2009). Washington, DC: Families USA.

Packard, M. D., & Reno, V. P. (1989). A look at very early retirees. *Social Security Bulletin, 52*(3), 16–29.

Pollitz, K., & Sorian, R. (2002). Ensuring health security: Is the individual market ready for prime time? *Health Affairs*, Web Exclusive.

Polsky, D., Doshi, J., Escarce, J., Manning, W., Paddock, S., Cen, L., et al. (2009). The health effects of Medicare for the near-elderly uninsured. *Health Services Research, 44*(3), 926–945.

Rust, J., & Phelan, C. (1997). How Social Security and Medicare affect retirement behavior in a world of incomplete markets. *Econometrica, 65*(4), 781–831.

Schoen, C., Collins, S. R., Kriss, J. L., & Doty, M. M. (2008). How many are underinsured? Trends among U.S. adults, 2003 and 2007. *Health Affairs*, Web Exclusive.

Schoen, C., & DesRoches, C. (2000). Uninsured and unstably insured: The importance of continuous insurance coverage. *Health Services Research, 35*(1, pt 2), 187–206.

Shen, Y.-C., & Long, S. K. (2006). What's driving the downward trend in employer-sponsored health insurance? *Health Services Research, 41*(6), 2074–2096.

Short, P. F., Shea, D. G., & Powell, M. P. (2001). *Health insurance on the way to Medicare: Is special government assistance warranted?* New York, NY: The Commonwealth Fund.

Sudano, J. J., & Baker, D. W. (2003). Intermittent lack of health insurance coverage and use of preventive services. *American Journal of Public Health, 93*(1), 130–137.

Swartz, K., & Stevenson, B. (2001). Health insurance coverage of people in the ten years before Medicare eligibility. In *Ensuring health and income security for an aging workforce.* Kalamazoo, MI: W.E. Upjohn Institute for Employment Research.

Vistnes, J., Cooper, P., Bernard, D., & Banthin, J. (2009). *Near-elderly adults, ages 55–64: Health insurance coverage, cost and access; estimates from the Medical Expenditure Panel Survey.* Rockville, MD: Agency for Health Care Policy and Research.

Weller, C. E., Wenger, J., & Gould, E. (2004a). Retiree health insurance coverage in an era of declining access to employer-sponsored insurance. *Journal of Aging and Social Policy, 18*(2), 11–30.

Weller, C. E., Wenger, J., & Gould, E. (2004b). *Health insurance coverage in retirement.* Washington, DC: Economic Policy Institute.

Zawacki, A. (2006). *Using the MEPS-IC to study retiree health insurance.* Washington, DC: U.S. Bureau of the Census.

The (Interconnected) Reasons Elder Americans File Consumer Bankruptcy

DEBORAH THORNE, PhD

Associate Professor of Sociology, Ohio University, Athens, Ohio, USA

Since the early 1990s, the age distribution of the bankruptcy population has shifted. Specifically, the age distribution curve has flattened, due in large part to an increase in the number of elder Americans (65 and older) who are filing bankruptcy. To date, the reasons for elder bankruptcies have not been studied. Quantitative and qualitative data from 381 elder bankruptcy respondents who participated in the 2007 Consumer Bankruptcy Project suggest that overwhelming interest and fees on credit cards, illnesses and injuries, income problems, aggressive debt collectors, and housing problems are the leading reasons that elder debtors file bankruptcy. Further, the vast majority of elder bankruptcies result not from a single cause, but rather from multiple interconnected causes.

INTRODUCTION

Every year since 1996, the number of petitions for consumer bankruptcy has hovered between 1 million and 1.5 million (American Bankruptcy Institute, 2009).[1] And while the number of annual household ︠lings has held relatively

---

The 2007 Consumer Bankruptcy Project data collection was supported by funding from the Robert Wood Johnson Foundation, the American Association of Retired Persons, the Federal Deposit Insurance Corporation, the University of Michigan, and Harvard Law School. The 2007 Consumer Bankruptcy Project was the joint effort of multiple scholars. The author thanks her coresearchers, professors Melissa Jacoby, Robert Lawless, Angela Littwin, Katherine Porter, John Pottow, and Elizabeth Warren and Drs. David Himmelstein, Teresa Sullivan, and Stef e Woolhandler for the hard work and thoughtful ideas that helped build a database that we could all use.

constant for well over a decade, the age distribution of petitioners has shifted. For example, in the early 1990s, petitioners at the tails of the distribution, the very young and very old, were much less likely to le bankruptcy than their indebted counterparts who were in their middle-age years (35 to 55). Several recent studies, however, conclude that the bankruptcy distribution curve has attened considerably, primarily because the population of lers has aged. Existing literature also suggests that because the bankruptcy population is aging at a considerably faster rate than the U.S. population generally, it re ects increasing nancial distress among older Americans rather than changing demographics.

What is missing from the literature, however, is an explanation of *why* older Americans are ling bankruptcy. Analyses of quantitative and qualitative data from the 2007 Consumer Bankruptcy Project reveal the ve leading reasons that elder debtors, those 65 and older, le bankruptcy: overwhelming interest and fees on credit cards, illnesses and injuries, income problems, aggressive debt collectors, and housing problems. The data also suggest that the majority of elder bankruptcies result from multiple interrelated crises, rather than a single unfortunate event.

THE AGING BANKRUPTCY POPULATION

For an increasing number of older Americans, nancial collapse is an unfortunate component of their golden years. People aged 65 and older are, more than ever before, likely to nd themselves in bankruptcy court (Flynn & Bermant, 2002; Golmant & Ulrich, 2007; Thorne, Warren, & Sullivan, 2008, 2009). Thorne et al. (2009) describe how, since 1991, the median age gap between the bankrupt and U.S. populations has continued to expand; while the average age for Americans has crept up only 3 percentage points to 36.1 years, the average age of the bankruptcy population has increased from 36.5 to 43 years (Figure 1).

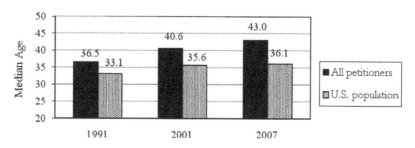

FIGURE 1 Median age, all bankruptcy petitioners and U.S. population, 1991, 2001, and 2007.

Source: Thorne, Warren, & Sullivan, 2009.

In this same study, the authors conclude that between 1991 and 2007, bankruptcy petitioners aged 65 to 74 experienced a relative increase in l- ing of 177.8%. Speci cally, in 1991, only 1.8% of those ling bankruptcy were aged 65 to 74, but by 2007, that proportion had climbed to 5.0%. Their ndings also suggest an increase in the rate of older lers among the U.S. population. In 1991, Americans aged 65 to 74 years led at a rate of 1.2 per 1,000; by 2007, that rate had increased to 2.7 per 1,000. The aging among Americans ling bankruptcy is re ected in the attening of the age distribution in Figure 2.

Reasons for Bankruptcy

Research that explores the reasons for bankruptcy has focused on the general, rather than the elder, bankruptcy population. Scholars have suggested that among the general bankruptcy population, illness and injury are leading causes of bankruptcy (Himmelstein, Warren, Thorne, & Woolhandler, 2005; Himmelstein, Thorne, Warren, & Woolhandler, 2009). Warren and Tyagi (2003) describe the "big three" reasons for bankruptcy as job loss, medical problems, and divorce or separation. Warren (2002) asserts that increased numbers of children are closely correlated with an increased likelihood of ling bankruptcy, especially among single female–headed households. To date, however, reasons for elder bankruptcies have not been explored. The results described in this article will begin to ll that void.

METHODS AND SAMPLE

Methods

From February to April 2007, the Consumer Bankruptcy Project collected names and addresses from a random national sample of approximately

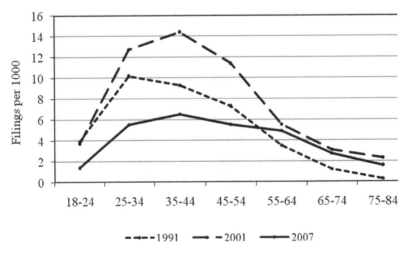

FIGURE 2 Bankruptcy ling rates per 1,000 U.S. population by age, 1991, 2001, and 2007.

5,000 recently bankrupt households.[2] Respondents completed and returned 2,314 questionnaires. Hereafter, these cases are referred to as the "general bankruptcy sample." Corresponding court records, which included extensive nancial data such as income, debts, and assets, were coded. All results discussed in this article come from analysis of questionnaire and court record data. From the general bankruptcy sample, 189 respondents reported that the petitioner (or petitioner's spouse, in the case of a joint ling) was 65 or older.[3]

During the same time frame, a supplemental sample of older Americans (65 and older) was drawn from a random national sample of approximately 8,500 bankruptcy lers. Because bankruptcy petitions do not include debtors' ages, research assistants used a public background check Web site to establish debtors' ages. Names and addresses were compared to determine whether the petitioner (or petitioner's spouse, in the case of joint lings) was 65 or older.[4] There were approximately 6 per 100 petitions wherein one petitioner was at least 65. Of the approximately 500 questionnaires that were mailed to elder lers, 217 were completed and returned. Of those, 192 con rmed that at least one petitioner was 65 or older; corresponding court records were coded.

To test for response bias, nancial variables from the court records of the general bankruptcy sample and 100 nonrespondent debtors were analyzed and compared. There were no signi cant differences between respondents and nonrespondents on the leading nancial variables, suggesting no response bias. Because respondents' ages are not listed on the bankruptcy petitions, no similar test for response bias could be made with the supplemental sample.

Sample

The "elder sample," which is the basis of this article, totals 381 cases wherein at least one petitioner was 65 or older: 189 elder cases came from the general bankruptcy sample and 192 cases came from the supplemental sample.[5]

AGE AND SEX

Median age of elder debtors was 71 years. Among those living alone, 66% were women and 34% were men.

MARITAL AND PARTNERSHIP STATUS

At the time of bankruptcy, about half (49.1%) of the elder respondents lived with a spouse or partner. This closely mirrors the general bankruptcy sample: 51.3% of respondents lived with a spouse or partner.

HOMEOWNERSHIP

Six in ten (59.7%) elder respondents owned their homes at the time of bankruptcy. Another third (34.0%) rented, while the remaining respondents (6.4%) reported "other" living arrangements. However, 68.8% of the elder respondents indicated that they had owned a home within the past 5 years. Thus, there was just slightly more than a 9 percentage point drop in home-ownership in the 5 years before the bankruptcy. Why did this happen? The data suggest that elder debtors did not voluntarily leave their homes, but instead confronted nancial circumstances that forced them out: of the elder respondents who had owned a home in the previous 5 years, 13% had lost their homes in foreclosure, deeded them back to the bank because of nancial dif culties, or sold them for nancial reasons.

Among the general bankruptcy sample, 65.7% had owned homes in the previous 5 years, but by the time of bankruptcy, the proportion of home-owners dropped 14.7 percentage points to 51.0%. Again, data suggest that the decline in homeownership was a matter of nancial necessity: 23.3% of the general bankruptcy sample that had owned a home in the 5 years prior to bankruptcy had lost it in foreclosure, deeded it back to the bank because of nancial dif culties, or sold it for nancial reasons. In 2007, 68.4% of the U.S. population owned their homes—comparable to the 68.8% of the elder sample and 65.7% of the general bankruptcy sample that owned homes 5 years before ling.

FINANCIAL CIRCUMSTANCES

In 2007, among American households in which head of household was aged 65 to 74, median annual income was $39,000 (Bucks, Kennickell, Mach, & Moore, 2009). That same year, annual household income of the general bankruptcy sample was $27,186. In contrast, median annual house-hold income for elder bankrupt debtors was only $23,280 (Table 1).

Not only did elder debtors have lower incomes, they also had more total and relative unsecured debt, such as credit card bills and medical bills. Their unsecured debts totaled $33,340—about $400 more than debtors in the general bankruptcy sample and approximately double that of nonbankrupt Americans. Further, elder debtors' unsecured debt was a much greater pro-portion of their annual incomes; they owed 1.4 times their annual incomes in unsecured debts, whereas respondents in the general bankruptcy sample owed 1.2 times their annual incomes. This is in stark contrast to both the general and elder U.S. populations whose unsecured debts were approx-imately one-third of their incomes. In contrast to the other three groups, elder debtors are carrying less mortgage debt; however, this is primarily a re ection of the modest values of their homes.

TABLE 1 Comparison of U.S. Population, General Bankruptcy Sample, and Elder Sample on Relevant Financial Measures

	U.S. population[1]	U.S. head of household 65–74[1]	General bankruptcy sample[2]	Elder bankruptcy sample[2]
Median annual income	$47,300	$39,000	$27,186	$23,280
Median unsecured debt[3]	$16,000	$13,300	$32,924	$33,340
Median mortgage debt	$107,000	$69,000	$92,750	$52,816
Value of primary residence	$200,000	$200,000	$111,424	$86,350

Note. [1]Source: Bucks et al. (2009).
[2]Source: Dollar amounts calculated from data from the Consumer Bankruptcy Project 2007.
[3]Median unsecured debt for the U.S. population and U.S. elder population combines installment loans (which include student loans) and credit card balances (Bucks et al., 2009). For both bankruptcy samples, unsecured debt is a total of all debt listed on Schedule F of the court records. While the variables used to construct unsecured debt for the U.S. and bankruptcy populations are not identical, they are similar and are presented here for purposes of general comparison.

Variables

An "illness or injury" reason for bankruptcy was designated if respondents indicated any one of the following on the questionnaire: (1) medical or health care bills were a reason for bankruptcy, or (2) out-of-pocket medical bills in the 2 years before bankruptcy were greater than $5,000 or were greater than 10% of household annual income,[6] or (3) the respondent remortgaged his or her home to pay for medical expenses, or (4) the respondent or the respondent's spouse or partner missed 2 weeks or more of work because of illness or injury, or (5) the respondent or the respondent's spouse or partner missed 2 weeks or more of work to care for a sick family member, or (6) the respondent or the respondent's spouse or partner was completely disabled and unable to work, or (7) the respondent said that medical problems of self, spouse, or another family member were a reason for bankruptcy.[7]

An "income problem" reason for bankruptcy was designated if respondents indicated any one of the following on the questionnaire: (1) the respondent or the respondent's spouse or partner lost at least 2 weeks of work-related income because they (a) were laid off or red, (b) were ill or injured, (c) took time off to care for a sick family member, or (d) any other reason; or (2) the respondent or the respondent's spouse or partner was not employed and seeking work or not employed and unable to work; or (3) the respondent indicated that a reason for bankruptcy was a decline in income, nancial problems that resulted from being self-employed, or an illness or injury that caused the respondent or the respondent's spouse or partner to miss 2 weeks or more of work.[8]

A "housing problem" reason for bankruptcy was designated if respondents indicated on the questionnaire that any one of the following were reasons for ling: (1) the mortgage payments increased beyond what the respondent could afford, or (2) the respondent wanted to re nance the mortgage to lower the payments but could not, or (3) a lender threatened to foreclose on the home.

The two remaining variables, "overwhelming credit card interest and fees" and "aggressive debt collection," were also options on the question-naire and were noncomposite variables.[9]

FINDINGS: REASONS FOR ELDER BANKRUPTCY

Bankruptcy scholars report that older Americans are increasingly likely to le bankruptcy, but we do not know why this is the case. To ll that gap in the literature, this article uses data from the 2007 Consumer Bankruptcy Project to describe the ve leading reasons older Americans le bankruptcy. The two most common reasons for elder debtors' bankruptcies are (1) over-whelming interest rates and fees from credit cards and (2) illness and injury (Figure 3). However, a considerable percentage of elder debtors led because of income problems, aggressive debt collectors, and housing problems.

High Interest and Fees on Credit Cards

The majority of the elder sample entered young adulthood 40 to 60 years ago—near the end of World War II and the beginning of the Vietnam War. In those days, there were usury laws and credit was not as readily available. How times have changed. Americans of all ages are ooded with offers for credit cards[10]—and interest rates often surpass 30%, with late-payment and over-limit fees exceeding $30.

Research that focuses speci cally on older Americans suggests that they are especially burdened by credit card debt. For example, Garcia and Draut

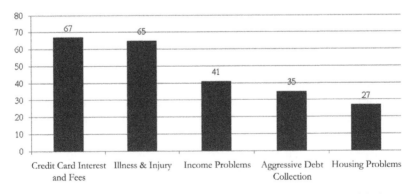

FIGURE 3 Reasons for elder bankruptcy, by percentage (respondents could choose more than one reason for their bankruptcy; therefore, percentages will not total 100%).

Source: Figure created from data from the Consumer Bankruptcy Project 2007.

(2009) report that between 2005 and 2008, the average amount of credit card debt carried by Americans 65 and older increased 26%—from $8,138 to $10,235. Comparatively, elder bankruptcy respondents are experiencing even more nancial strain. Their median unsecured debt, which includes credit card bills as well as other short-term debts such as medical bills, is $33,340. Given this debt load and their limited incomes, it is not surprising that 67% of elder respondents indicated that a reason for bankruptcy was that "interest and fees on credit cards were overwhelming."

The statistical data, however, provide only one piece of the puzzle. Another powerful data point that helped situate the reasons for bankruptcy was the back of the questionnaire where respondents were asked to "tell their story." A 74-year-old married man described the ways in which a xed income, increasing everyday expenses, and credit card interest combined to cause his nancial collapse:

> I know that I had to go bankrupt because [I was] on a x[ed] income, and in ation [was] stead[il]y going up and my income was not. The prices of gasoline and grocer[ies] and medicine bill[s were] going up. And when I couldn't pay my credit cards on time, the interest rate tripled and skyrocketed. So, therefore, I was in a x and had to go bankrupt.

An 83-year-old widow spoke directly to the amount of interest she was being charged when she wrote: "[I] could not keep up with medical and health care and living needs and make payments on credit cards charging 32% interest. [I had] limited retirement income."

Another widow in her early 80s described the nancial implications of falling behind on credit card payments:

> [I was] overwhelmed with credit card fees and charges. [I] made minimum payments and just got further and further in debt. [It was] impossible to get out of it. The credit card companies started taking payments directly out of my checking account, leaving me nothing to pay rent and other essentials. [I] started bouncing checks, not realizing they were taking out more and more often unauthorized. [I] became $95,000 in debt with nothing to show for it. My children had to pay my lot rent [for my mobile home] and utilities.

Fixed incomes virtually mandate xed expenses. However, when credit card interest and fees increase rapidly and unexpectedly, elder debtors often nd themselves unable to keep pace. In short order, they are in a nancial hole so deep that it would be virtually impossible for them to dig out.

Illness and Injury

There is convincing evidence that the link between medical problems and bankruptcy has increased signi cantly since 2001. Speci cally, the

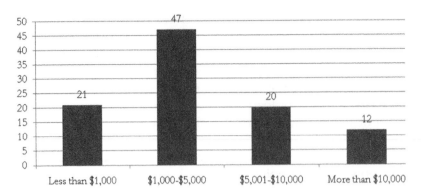

FIGURE 4 Amount of out-of-pocket medical expenses 2 years before bankruptcy, by percentage.

Source: Figure created from data from the Consumer Bankruptcy Project 2007.

percentage of medical bankruptcies rose from 46.2% in 2001 to 62.1% in 2007 (Himmelstein et al., 2009). And while Himmelstein et al. (2009) do not disaggregate their ndings by age, they do report that medical debtors were signi cantly older than nonmedical debtors. Other research suggests that even for retirement-aged Americans who are Medicare-eligible, medical expenses are often staggering. McGee (2008) reported that 65-year-old couples who retired in 2008 could expect to pay out-of-pocket medical expenses and Medicare premiums of $12,000 to $15,000 annually, or a total of about $225,000 by their 80th birthdays.

Data from the elder lers suggest that medical expenses may have hit them particularly hard. The costs associated with illness and injury were a reason for almost two-thirds (65%) of elder bankruptcies—which is disconcerting because this population is eligible for Medicare. Among elder lers who indicated an illness or injury reason for bankruptcy, 89% were responsible for out-of-pocket medical care or prescription expenses in the 2 years before bankruptcy. As Figure 4 illustrates, the majority of these debtors (47%) spent between $1,000 and $5,000 on out-of-pocket medical expenses over these 2 years.[11] And while this may not sound like an exorbitant amount, on a monthly basis this extracts anywhere from $42 to $208 from elder debtors. Further, almost one-third (32%) of elder debtors paid more than $5,000 in out-of-pocket medical expenses, which is almost one-quarter of their pretax income. Undoubtedly, these out-of-pocket medical expenses will cause considerable nancial strain.

Debtors' stories revealed how costly health care could be and how often they had little choice but to charge it to their credit cards. An 80-year-old widower described his situation:

Ins[urance] premiums, [prescription] expenses, plus non-covered items were around $10,000 per year. I used credit card advances, etc., and never was late making payments. The last 2 years, they raised the interest rate as high as 24.99%. I tried to discuss it [with credit card lenders] but was told that the number of accounts and balances caused the rate increase. My credit report showed no late payments. In order to keep from depleting my IRA, I chose to le bankruptcy.

This explanation from a 70-year-old retiree exposed the catastrophic correlation between illness and losing one's job:

I am/was the only one employed in the family. [In] December 2004, I got ill and was hospitalized for 1 week. My family decided and convinced me against my will not to go back to work due to my age and deteriorating health. I resigned [in] January 2005 without the bene t of workman's compensation or pension.

These stories depict the interconnectedness between the reasons for bankruptcy. In the rst example, the respondent describes how unmanageable medical expenses swiftly translated into credit card debt. The second story illustrates the cascading effects of an illness—because the respondent was unwell, he had to quit work, and the resulting decline in income pushed him into bankruptcy.

Income Decline

A decline in income was a reason for just over 40% of elder bankruptcies. While a few respondents had chosen to retire and had outlived their retirement accounts, most said that they preferred to continue working. Some were unemployed because of age discrimination. An 85-year-old widow said she was "let go" because of her age. And once she lost her job, things began to unravel—repaying medical expenses that she charged to her credit card was virtually impossible:

Our problems began when my spouse entered a facility for substance abuse (alcoholic) [which] was paid [for] by credit card ($16,000). As cost and spending accelerated, credit card payments were kept under control until I was let go from employment because of age. Medical bills continued to rise when my spouse entered a wound care center for the past 2 years. . . . We elected to le bankruptcy 6 months ago to get relief.

Other respondents insisted that their age made nding *new* jobs dif cult. A 67-year-old man who was laid off believed that his age was the reason he could not nd subsequent employment:

I did not really plan to le bankruptcy because I am ashamed to be ridiculed by my colleagues, coworkers, and relatives. . . . I am getting old and nobody wants to hire [me] anymore. I had to make the hardest decision in my life—that is to le bankruptcy.

More common were elder respondents for whom medical problems caused unemployment and declines in income. A 75-year-old woman was fired following an essential surgery; unfortunately, even after regaining her health, she was unable to find employment.

> I am a senior citizen (75) who now finds herself in a most distressing situation. Prior to bankruptcy, I had been on my job 13 years. It was necessary that I take a month's medical leave to have hip replacement surgery due to severe arthritis. After surgery, I went into a nursing home for rehab. On my 19th day of sick leave, my employer came to the nursing home and fired me—in front of witnesses; needless to say, deep depression ensued. Two days after my release I began (and am continuing) my search for a job. I received unemployment compensation for a few months but have been denied all other sources [of] state assistance. My social security check covers my mortgage, phone, lights, and car insurance, but it leaves very little for credit card payments, doctor visits, prescriptions, medical insurance payments, and vet expenses (extremely necessary) for my 14-year-old little dog. I have cut my personal and household expenses to the bone, but am still worried as to my future, if I can't find a job.

Finally, a 73-year-old woman described how her husband's stroke resulted in both of them being unemployed:

> My husband had a stroke May 2, 2006. We lost our jobs because of it. He had three jobs and I had one before his stroke. [She quit work to care for him.] We had planned on getting all our bills paid up in 4 years. We were deeply in debt. We now only have our Social Security to live on. My husband cannot talk and I have cancer.

The elders' stories reiterate the correlation between the leading reasons for bankruptcy as they describe a vortex of financial problems: credit card debt, medical expenses, and inadequate or declining incomes. Their stories also suggest that age discrimination may intensify their income problems. Regardless of the reasons for their bankruptcies, the fact is that many elder debtors would prefer to continue to work, and they often do so until their bodies give out.

Aggressive Debt Collectors

When the Fair Debt Collection Practices Act was amended in 2006, it included a statement that read: "There is abundant evidence of the use of abusive, deceptive, and unfair debt collection practices by many debt collectors. Abusive debt collection practices contribute to the number of personal bankruptcies. . . ." (2006, p. 2). In her classic work on emotional labor, Hochschild (1983, p. 139) describes how bill collectors are trained to humiliate debtors by suggesting that they are "lazy and of low moral character." Debt collectors are also persistent, often calling numerous times a day. Thus, it is no surprise that for more than one-third (35%) of elder debtors, aggressive debt collection was a reason for their bankruptcies. A 65-year-old widow stated that when she became delinquent on her credit card payments, the collectors began to harass her.

> I had a stroke last July. I didn't want to do this [le bankruptcy]. . . .
> I cashed in all my 401(k)s to pay my bills. That about killed me. I
> need that money to survive. But my creditors, the credit card compa-
> nies, were harassing me so bad. I asked them to help me and they said
> they couldn't. They said that I charged the bills so I should pay them.
> But how do you live on $10 a week? That's all I have left over for food.
> I didn't want to do this but I had no choice. And I found a part-time
> job, but they let all of us who are over 65 go. They know that we get
> sick. They'd rather have people who are 20-something than old peo-
> ple. . . . It's rough on people. At 65 years old, I never thought I'd be
> ling bankruptcy. I never thought I'd have to do this.

According to an 84-year-old woman, collectors for MBNA relied on threats as a way to collect on the debt:

> I lost my vision and had open heart surgery and back surgery. These are
> things you just can't prepare for. My husband had a [credit card] account
> through the Masons that was sold to MBNA. They were very nasty to
> me and threatened to do bad things to me if I didn't come up with the
> money. They wouldn't work with us and because of my poor health we
> had no choice but to le for bankruptcy. My husband just had a biopsy
> for a growth on his lung.

Frequent collection calls, even if non-aggressive, were often so stressful that debtors sought bankruptcy protection. A 71-year-old married woman wrote:

> We always made our payments timely but due to having back surgery
> and [being] able to work only part-time it was so hard to live. . . . We
> were getting calls every day from credit card companies (3) and the stress
> was too much. We didn't know anything else to do because we did not
> want to bother our children.

Finally, if "aggressive collection efforts" and "high interest rates and fees" are collapsed into a single reason for bankruptcy, the result is that 73% of elder respondents led for one of these two reasons—*making this combined answer the single most common reason for filing bankruptcy*. This suggests that the products and practices of the lending industry are the chief factors driving many elder Americans into bankruptcy.

Housing Problems

In 2007, rates of home foreclosures skyrocketed to unprecedented levels. While homeowners of all ages were obviously affected, elder debtors were hit particularly hard: More than one-quarter (27%) of elder respondents indicated that housing problems were a reason for their bankruptcy. A recurrent story was that mortgage payments outstripped incomes. For some, this occurred because of adjustable rate mortgages. While describing the implications of his adjustable rate mortgage, a 69-year-old retired police of cer also revealed the complex relationship among mortgage expenses, health insurance, and credit cards:

> My mortgage payment went up with this adjustable rate mortgage and I didn't understand how it worked. . . . I have owned my home for 6 years and the school taxes alone are now $3,700 a year. Also after retiring I had health insurance for 4 years and then I lost it. So now I am paying over $400 for health insurance coverage. The credit card companies are vultures. If you are 1 day late the penalties they charge are very high. The interest rates go up and the fees and penalties are added and it is too hard to get caught up. Creditors were calling me at one time constantly every day.

A quote from a 65-year-old licensed practical nurse illustrates how an illness can lead to late mortgage payments:

> I had a stroke and a ve bypass surgery and I have been unable to work. I had just bought a house and had to put it in bankruptcy. I may still lose my home because I just keep falling behind on my bills. I get Social Security and it just don't go far enough.

For those of us not yet in our elder years, the thought of losing our home is likely quite stressful. But imagine being elderly, possibly having lived in your home for decades, and then losing it, along with all of the equity, in foreclosure. When elder Americans are forced from their homes, where do they go? With rising rents and declining retirement income, can they afford new housing? Or do they become part of our homeless population?

Bankruptcy's Con ated Causes

It would be ideal if we could know which *single* event caused elder debtors' bankruptcies. But the reality is that bankruptcy tends to be untidy and complex, and the reasons for ling seldom stand alone. As the qualitative data demonstrate, bankruptcy more often results from a cascade of crucial events—an illness or injury leads to a job loss, which leads to late mortgage and credit card payments, which result in higher interest rates, and, eventually, the collection calls begin.

Quantitative data paint a similar picture: Multiple crises were behind more than 7 in 10 (71%) elder bankruptcies. Fewer than one-quarter (22%) of elder bankruptcies were caused by a single event, and a slight 8% of elder respondents indicated that their bankruptcies resulted from something *other than* one of the ve reasons discussed in this article (Figure 5).

Taken together, the qualitative and quantitative data make a strong case for the interconnectedness of the reasons for elder bankruptcy. No single event is to blame. Instead, there is a chorus of reasons, but the end result is still the same.

DISCUSSION

Compared with their counterparts in 1991, older Americans who led bankruptcy in 2007 made up a greater proportion of the bankruptcy population and, among the U.S. population, their rates of ling increased (Thorne et al., 2008, 2009). For the tens of thousands of elder Americans who le for bankruptcy each year, the golden years appear to have lost some of their sparkle. But why are so many older Americans seeking refuge from their creditors in bankruptcy court?[12] The data presented here suggest that they are collapsing under excessive credit card interest and fee charges, unmanageable medical expenses, boorish treatment from the lending industry, income problems, and an inability to stay current on their mortgage payments.

Further, it appears that there is seldom a single reason for their bankruptcies; instead, elder debtors often le because of the cascading effects of multiple interrelated life crises, each as consequential as the last.

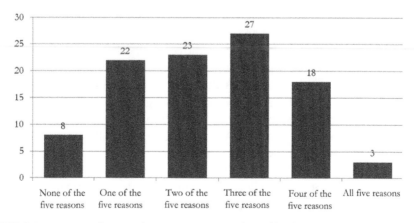

FIGURE 5 Percentage of respondents reporting number of leading reasons for bankruptcy.

Source: Figure created from data from the Consumer Bankruptcy Project 2007.

And while the interrelatedness of the reasons for elder bankruptcy makes the remedies more complex, there are some steps that could be taken to reduce the likelihood of nancial collapse among older Americans.

In May 2009, President Obama signed into law the Credit Card Accountability Responsibility and Disclosure Act of 2009. The reforms are expected to provide borrowers protection from some of the most predatory lending practices such as universal default, double-cycle billing, and increasing the interest rate on preexisting balances (The Credit Card Accountability Responsibility and Disclosure Act of 2009, 2009). While these changes will protect Americans across the board, they are likely to be especially bene cial for older Americans who are struggling with credit card debt and who have xed and limited incomes. Given that so many elder debtors stated speci - cally that sharply increasing interest rates on preexisting balances propelled them into bankruptcy, changes resulting from the Credit Card Accountability Responsibility and Disclosure Act may well go a long way toward keeping them out of bankruptcy.

A related reason for elder bankruptcies is aggressive tactics used by debt collectors. The Fair Debt Collection Practices Act explicitly prohibits harassment, threats, use of obscene language, and repeatedly calling the debtor with the intent to annoy or harass. However, the act applies only to collection attorneys and debt collection companies, not to the original creditors (e.g., the credit card company). Given the stories from elder debtors describing harassing and threatening collection calls from speci cally MBNA, a potential remedy may be to extend the Fair Debt Collection Practices Act to original creditors.

Older Americans came of age when bankers would not lend more than they believed a borrower could repay; thus, they may also be exceptionally trusting of lenders and therefore vulnerable to predatory lending. To that end, one solution might lie with the proposed Consumer Financial Protection Agency. This agency, conceptualized by Warren (2007) as an agency on the side of the consumer rather than the corporation, would work to ensure that lenders' contract terms are transparent and would "eliminate the hidden tricks and traps" that make some credit products dangerous for consumers.

The literature on the relationship between bankruptcy and medical problems consistently concludes that illness and injury are leading causes of bankruptcy, regardless of the debtor's age (Himmelstein et al., 2009). However, older Americans are uniquely vulnerable to the costs associated with health care. The fact that American couples will average $225,000 on out-of-pocket medical expenses between ages 65 and 80 partly explains their circumstances (McGee, 2008). But also problematic is that recovering from medical debt is especially dif cult for older Americans. Realistically, they may not be physically able to work. And if they are able, they may confront age discrimination, as illustrated by the quotes in this article.

It is especially troubling that, because of inadequate and xed incomes, elder debtors are charging medical expenses to their credit cards, selling their homes, and taking money from their savings or retirement accounts. In the long term, these options are futile, and none is acceptable. Elders are tapping out already miniscule resources and still winding up in bankruptcy court, nancially vulnerable, asset-broke, and potentially homeless. Weller, Wenger, and Gould (2006, p. 12) make a similar observation about the effects of health care costs on retirement assets: "Retirement income security has also been undermined by rising health care costs as health insurance costs and medical care in ation simultaneously grew."

The results reported in this article suggest yet another factor that leaves older Americans exceptionally susceptible to overwhelming medical debt: the unfortunate reality that medical problems are frequently part and parcel of our later years. These medical problems, while still very expensive, are not necessarily end-of-life catastrophic illnesses. They are better described as routine and chronic. For example, back surgeries, osteoporosis, heart disease, lung disease, and cancers, as well as their concomitant prescription medications, appear to be unaffordable and often propel elder debtors into bankruptcy. Further, elder debtors' comments suggest that their health insurance, whether private or Medicare, is inadequate to meet the costs of the later-life chronic illnesses. The relationship between later-life illnesses and nancial collapse, as well as what appears to be inadequate insurance coverage among elder debtors, are pressing issues that beg further study.

Steps should also be taken to ensure that older Americans are able to work as long as they wish and that they retire with adequate and protected retirement incomes. Stricter enforcement of age discrimination laws may improve the nancial circumstances of some older Americans and thereby reduce the likelihood that they will nd themselves in bankruptcy. Further, the retirement income of older Americans must be protected and buffered from market upheavals. Movement toward individual accounts leaves all people, but especially retirees, exceptionally vulnerable during economic downturns. Tragically, Weller and Wenger (2009) report that with the recent recession and declining stock prices, retirement income security was "decimated."

Older Americans are a unique population. While they are not necessarily chronically poor, they are often at risk. Their limited and xed incomes leave them particularly vulnerable when confronted with credit tricks, health problems, and income shocks. Admittedly, the reasons for bankruptcy among this population are complex, and as such, the solutions will require considerable thought and determination. However, the increasing rate of bankruptcy lings among our oldest citizens is an ethical issue that we, as a country, must address and reverse. To ignore this social dilemma would be a national disgrace.

NOTES

1. The years from 2005 through 2007 were anomalous because the law changed signi cantly with the adoption of the Bankruptcy Abuse Prevention and Consumer Protection Act. The act took effect in October 2005, and that year, in anticipation of changes in the law, more than two million households rushed the bankruptcy courts. For the next 2 years, lings remained below one million; however, by 2008, the number of households ling bankruptcy rebounded and again topped one million.

2. The random national sample was provided by Mike Bickford and his colleagues at AACER (Automated Access to Court Electronic Records), an Oklahoma City–based bankruptcy data and management company.

3. For a complete description of data collection methods, see Lawless et al. (2008, pp. 391–398).

4. For many cases, there were exact matches on both name and address. For others, there were exact name matches but different addresses. A protocol was established to deal with these "possible" age hits; for example, if the debtor had an uncommon name but the address was in the same county, the case was counted and a questionnaire was mailed.

5. Results from a Mann-Whitney test for signi cance revealed no difference between elder respondents from the general bankruptcy sample or the supplemental sample on key economic variables such as income, assets, or debt.

6. Out-of-pocket medical expenses were measured in ranges: less than $1,000; $1,000 to $5,000; $5,001 to $10,000, and more than $10,000. Midrange out-of-pocket medical expenses were used to determine whether medical bills exceeded 10% of annual income. For example, debtors in the rst range with medical expenses of less than $1,000 were assigned a midrange medical expense of $500. If household annual income was less than $5,000, medical expenses thereby exceeded 10% of income and these cases were coded as having an "illness or injury" reason for bankruptcy. Debtors in the second range, $1,000 to $5,000, had a midrange medical expense of $2,500. If these households had annual income of less than $25,000, medical expenses exceeded 10% of income and these cases were also coded as having an "illness or injury" reason for bankruptcy. Regardless of income, respondents with out-of-pocket medical expenses in the third ($5,001 to $10,000) or fourth (more than $10,000) ranges were coded as having an "illness or injury" reason for bankruptcy.

7. The "illness or injury" variable is constructed to mirror that used by Himmelstein et al. (2009), who also used data from the 2007 Consumer Bankruptcy Project to report on medical bankruptcies.

8. The "income problem" variable is constructed to mirror that used by Warren and Tyagi (2003), who reported results from the 2001 Consumer Bankruptcy Project in their book, *The Two-Income Trap*.

9. The questionnaire is reprinted in Lawless et al. (2008, pp. 399–402). Quantitative data came from closed-ended questions on the questionnaire. Qualitative data were gathered from the back page of the questionnaire, where respondents were given the opportunity to "tell their stories" and write about what had happened to them.

10. In 2007, U.S. consumers received 7.9 billion direct mail credit card solicitations. This does not include offers made in stores at the point of sale, over the telephone, or via the internet (Cardweb.com, 2007).

11. Debtors who reported spending less than $5,001 did not "qualify" as having an "illness or injury" reason for bankruptcy unless their out-of-pocket expenses were greater than 10% of their annual income. See footnote 6 for examples and a thorough explanation.

12. I do not want to overstate the magnitude of the problem. Of the bankrupt population, elder lers are less than 5%, and among the U.S. population, the rate of elder debtors ling for bankruptcy is approximately 2 per 1,000.

REFERENCES

American Bankruptcy Institute. (2009). *Annual business and non-business filings by year (1980–2008)*. Retrieved June 15, 2009, from http://www.abiworld.org/AM/AMTemplate.cfm?Section=Home&TEMPLATE=/CM/ContentDisplay.cfm&CONTENTID=57826.

Bucks, B. K., Kennickell, A. B., Mach, T. L., & Moore, K. B. (2009). *Changes in U.S. family finances from 2004 to 2007: Evidence from the Survey of Consumer Finances. Federal Reserve Bulletin.* Retrieved September 28, 2009, from http://www.federalreserve.gov/pubs/bulletin/2009/pdf/scf09.pdf.

Cardweb.com. (2007). *Orvis card (2/21/2007).* Retrieved June 20, 2009, from http://www.cardweb.com/cardtrak/news/2007/february/21a.html.

The Credit Card Accountability Responsibility and Disclosure Act of 2009. (2009). Retrieved June 23, 2009, from http://banking.senate.gov/public/index.cfm?FuseAction=Files.View&FileStore_id=721389f5-62b0-46b5-b855-85621d0a8d69.

The Fair Debt Collection Practices Act. (2006). Retrieved June 23, 2009, from http://www.ftc.gov/bcp/edu/pubs/consumer/credit/cre27.pdf.

Flynn, E., & Bermant, G. (2002). A closer look at elderly chapter 7 debtors. *American Bankruptcy Institute Law Journal, 21*(3). Retrieved December 6, 2009, from http://www.justice.gov/ust/eo/public_affairs/articles/docs/abi_042002.htm.

Garcia, J., & Draut, T. (2009). *The plastic safety net: How households are coping in a fragile economy.* Retrieved August 10, 2009, from http://demos.org/publication.cfm?currentpublicationID=C1B896F4-3FF4-6C82-56F2B3EF557CCFF5.

Golmant, J., & Ulrich, T. (2007). Aging and bankruptcy: The baby boomers meet up at bankruptcy court. *American Bankruptcy Institute Journal, 26*(4), 4.

Himmelstein, D. U., Thorne, D., Warren, E., & Woolhandler, S. (2009). Medical bankruptcy in the United States, 2007: Results of a national study. *The American Journal of Medicine.* Retrieved December 6, 2009, from http://www.pnhp.org/new_bankruptcy_study/Bankruptcy-2009.pdf.

Himmelstein, D. U., Warren, E., Thorne, D., & Woolhandler, S. (2005). Illness and injury as contributors to bankruptcy. *Health Affairs: The Policy Journal of the Health Sphere,* Web exclusive: February 2; w5-63–w5-75. Retrieved June 24, 2009, from http://content.healthaffairs.org/cgi/reprint/hlthaff.w5.63v1.

Hochschild, A. (1983). *The managed heart: Commercialization of human feeling.* Los Angeles, CA: University of California Press.

Lawless, R. M., Littwin, A. K., Porter, K. M., Pottow, J. A. E., Thorne, D. K., & Warren, E. (2008). Did bankruptcy reform fail? An empirical study of consumer debtors. *The American Bankruptcy Law Journal, 82*(3), 349–406.

McGee, S. (2008). The hidden costs of the golden years. *Barrons.* Retrieved June 17, 2009, from http://online.barrons.com/article/SB121401034714593887.html?mod=9_0031_b_this_weeks_magazine_main.

Thorne, D., Warren, E., & Sullivan, T. A. (2008). Generations of struggle. *AARP Public Policy Institute: Research Report, 11,* 1–13.

Thorne, D., Warren, E., & Sullivan, T. A. (2009). Bankruptcy's aging population. *Harvard Law and Policy Review, 3*(1), 87–101.

Warren, E. (2002). Bankrupt children. *Minnesota Law Review, 86,* 1003–1032.

Warren, E. (2007). Unsafe at any rate. *Democracy: A Journal of Ideas, 5.* Retrieved September 28, 2009, from http://www.democracyjournal.org/article.php?ID=6528.

Warren, E., & Tyagi, A. W. (2003). *The two-income trap: Why middle-class mothers and fathers are going broke.* New York: Basic Books.

Weller, C. E., & Wenger, J. B. (2009). What happens to de ned contribution accounts when labor markets and nancial markets move together? *Journal of Aging and Social Policy, 21*(3), 256–276.

Weller, C. E., Wenger, J. B., & Gould, E. (2006). A prescription for more retirement income security: Retiree health insurance coverage in an era of declining access to employer-sponsored insurance. *Journal of Aging and Social Policy, 18*(2), 11–30.

Reforming Retirement: Values and Self-Interest Drive Support for Policy Reform in Opposite Directions

DAVID MADLAND, PhD

Director, American Worker Project, Center for American Progress, Washington, DC, USA

Americans' attitudes about retirement policy reform are being pulled in two directions. Because of their worries about retirement security, individuals are likely to support greater government intervention. However, because of their belief in the value of self-reliance, individuals are likely to be concerned about government interventions in the economy. This paper explores the tension between self-interest and self-reliant values and examines how these factors affect attitudes about retirement policy, testing, with a unique private survey, the degree to which concern about retirement security leads self-interested Americans increasingly to support retirement policy reforms and those with self-reliant values to decrease support. The paper also attempts to tease out the conditions under which self-interest and self-reliant values exert greater or less influence on views about retirement policy. In doing so, the paper helps clarify the level of public support for retirement policy reform and indicates the types of policies likely to garner higher levels of support.

INTRODUCTION

To increase retirement savings, retirement experts and elected of cials have proposed a number of changes to the private retirement system in the

United States (Weller, 2008). The level of public support for such proposals is likely to be a factor determining whether the changes are enacted (Page & Shapiro, 1983). Public opinion about economic issues is shaped in large part by two forces, self-interest and political values (Hasenfeld & Rafferty, 1989); yet, for retirement policy, these forces are likely to pull in opposite directions. As a result, the degree to which self-interest and political values in uence attitudes is likely to determine the level of public support for retirement policy reforms.

The paper explores this tension between self-interest and self-reliant values by analyzing attitudes about changes to the private U.S. retirement system. The study examines whether self-interest and self-reliant values affect attitudes about retirement policy in a similar manner as they do for other social welfare policies, testing whether high levels of concern about retirement security are likely to lead self-interested Americans increasingly to support retirement policy reforms and whether Americans' self-reliant values reduce expectations about retirement policy reform. The paper also attempts to tease out the conditions under which self-interest and self-reliant values exert greater or less in uence on views about retirement policy. In doing so, the paper helps clarify the level of public support for retirement policy reform and indicates the types of policies likely to garner higher levels of support.

LITERATURE REVIEW

Retirement security is a signi cant concern for many Americans, with a majority of workers: "doubt[ing] they will have enough money to live comfortably once they retire" (Newport, 2009, p. 1). Retirement is the public's primary long-term economic worry after health care, and some polls indicate that Americans are even more worried about retirement than health care (Helman, Copeland, & VanDerhei, 2009; Teixeira, 2006, 2008; Jacobe, 2008; Madland, 2007; Almeida, Kenneally, & Madland, 2008).

Such strong concerns about retirement security are likely to lead to high levels of support for retirement policy reforms: Research about other economic policies nds that individuals are more likely to support reforms when they think current policies are insuf cient and believe they will bene t from the reform (Cook & Barrett, 1992; Hasenfeld & Rafferty, 1989; Ponza, Duncan, Concoran, & Groskind, 1989; Chong, Citrin, & Conley, 2001). In short, high levels of concern make individuals behave in a self-interested manner, and self-interested individuals are more likely to support policies that they think will bene t them personally.

While the level of concern about retirement security uctuates with economic conditions (Morin & Taylor, 2009; National Institute on Retirement Security, 2009), even if the economy signi cantly improves, it is likely that worries about retirement will remain relatively high: The public has expressed high levels of concern about retirement for many years, in good economic conditions and in poor conditions (Helman et al., 2009; Wright & Davies, 2007; *The Wall Street Journal*/NBC News, 1999; Yankelovich Inc., 2007). Thus, because of widespread concerns about retirement security, we might expect the public strongly to support policies to address this issue.

However, attitudes about social welfare policies are driven not only by self-interest but also, in large part, by political values. (Jaeger, 2006; Pereira & Van Ryzin, 1998; Hasenfeld & Rafferty, 1989; Feldman & Steenbergen, 2001). Political values in America are shaped by an ethic of self-reliance that is not especially conducive to supporting social welfare programs, such as policies to increase retirement security (McClosky & Zaller, 1984; Hartz, 1955; Schlozman & Verba, 1979).[1] Americans, it is often said, are characterized by a belief in the power of the individual to triumph over adversity. The American dream is to get ahead on your own.

For self-reliant Americans, individuals should be responsible for themselves, and government intervention is viewed as excusing citizens from their responsibilities and fostering inappropriate behavior among recipients. Individuals are morally responsible for taking care of themselves, and government interventions in the economy are wrong according to those with self-reliant values. In the self-reliant value system, "Economic success is a function of hard work and thrift" (Hasenfeld & Rafferty, 1989, p. 1030), while "government intervention is perceived to foster dependency and thus is morally corrupting." In short, for people with self-reliant values, government interventions in the economy are improper.

Thus, self-reliant values can be expected to reduce support for many reforms to the private sector because the policies are viewed as inappropriate. Self-reliant values can also reduce support for government interventions in the economy through the effect they have on expectations for the success of the policy (Hochschild, 1981; Gaventa, 1980). For people with self-reliant values, solutions that rely on others, and especially on the government, are often viewed as wasteful and as providing the wrong incentives and thus are unlikely to work.

While there is no absolute standard by which to judge whether a particular government intervention in the economy is likely to be perceived by people with self-reliant values as inappropriate, Americans tend to think that some types of government interventions are more consistent with their self-reliant values than others (Feldman & Zaller, 1992; Free & Cantril, 1968; Hasenfeld & Rafferty, 1989). As Hasenfeld and Rafferty (1989, p. 1042) argue, Americans are more likely to think that contributory programs like Social Security, where citizens earn bene ts "through their productive participation in society," are more consistent with their self-reliant values than other programs such as means-tested welfare bene ts. Further, incremental policy changes are often viewed as more acceptable than more major changes that involve a new role for government (Kingdon, 1995; Goss, 2006). As a result, policies that have strong contributory elements and require a relatively modest and familiar role for government are more likely than other types of government interventions in the economy to be perceived as consistent with self-reliant values.

Even when people support a particular economic policy, they generally have low expectations for its success if they think it conflicts with their self-reliant values (Madland, 2007). (People can support a solution but think it is unlikely to work. For example, during debates about President Bush's bank bailout plan and President Obama's stimulus bill, some people supported the plans, even though they were uncertain the efforts would succeed, because they thought the alternative of not doing anything would be worse.[2]) Even though people may want the government to do something about a problem, their self-reliant values make them think governmental solutions are unrealistic. As Hochschild (1981, p. 266) writes, such people often feel, "helpless, bitter, [and] resigned." In short, people with self-reliant values have low expectations for the success of government interventions in the economy. Thus, self-reliant values can reduce support for economic policies in two ways: by making some policies seem both inappropriate and unrealistic.

Little quantitative analysis has been done to separate out the two different ways in which self-reliant values can reduce policy support, making this study one of the first. However, research consistently finds that self-reliant values lower support for a range of economic policies (Blekesaune & Quadagno, 2003; Quadagno & Street, 2005; Cook & Barrett, 1992; Hasenfeld & Rafferty, 1989; Lane, 2001). This research has not focused on policies about the U.S. private retirement system, but we should expect that self-reliant values reduce support in this policy area.

No matter the state of the economy, people are likely to keep their self-reliant values. Sudden increases or decreases in wealth do not change people's basic views about the role of the individual in the economy, as studies of lottery winners, the unemployed, and those who have lost retirement benefits have found (Schlozman & Verba, 1979; Doherty, Gerber, & Green, 2006; Madland, 2007).

As important as self-interest and political values are in influencing public opinion about economic policy, they are not the only two factors that matter. Demographic factors and partisanship, which are often closely related to self-interest and political values, are known independently to impact policy views. Previous research indicates that women are more likely to prefer government intervention in the economy and thus are more likely to support retirement policy reforms, while wealthier and more educated people tend to prefer less government intervention in the economy and thus are less likely to support retirement policy reforms (Alvarez & McCaffery, 2003; Blekesaune & Quadagno, 2003; Cook & Barrett, 1992; Hasenfeld & Rafferty, 1989; Ponza et al., 1989). Young adults today are generally more supportive of government interventions in the economy than older Americans (Madland & Teixeira, 2009) and thus are more likely to support retirement policy reforms. In addition, people who identify with the Republican Party are less likely to support government intervention in the economy than those who identify with the Democratic Party and are thus less likely to support retirement policy reforms (Cook & Barrett, 1992; Hasenfeld & Rafferty, 1989).

In sum, theory suggests that public support for retirement policy reform is simultaneously pulled in two directions, with people's values and their self-interests in conflict. Because of worries about retirement security, self-interested individuals are likely to support greater government intervention. However, because of their self-reliant values, individuals are likely to be concerned about government interventions in the economy. As a result, Americans are likely to be torn between their desire to support specific retirement policy solutions and their general opposition to government intervention.[3]

METHODS

This study analyzes survey data to explore the impact of self-interest and self-reliant values on support for retirement policy change. It does so by testing how self-interest and self-reliant values affect the initial level of support expressed for a retirement policy reform and then by exploring how these factors affect expectations for the success of a retirement policy reform.

The survey data consisted of 804 registered voters and was conducted by Hart Research Associates, a private polling firm, in July 2006 (Hart Research Associates, 2006). Hart Research Associates is a leading U.S. survey research firm and has conducted well over 5,000 public opinion surveys over the past 3 decades (Hart Research Associates, 2009). The 2006 Hart poll is one of the most comprehensive surveys of American attitudes about retirement policy.

Table 1 presents the demographic, socioeconomic, and political characteristics of the sample of registered voters, which are closely in line with those of the politically active population. In the sample, a large majority of respondents were White (78%), while 8% were Hispanic, 7% were Black, 2% were Asian, and 6% were "other." Women constituted 55% of the sample, while men made up 45%. The median annual income was between $40,000 and $50,000, and the median age was between 50 and 54. Of the sample, 38% supported the Democratic Party, 30% the Republican Party, and 32% considered themselves independent. Sixty-six percent of respondents completed at least some college.

Voter exit polls from 2006—a more politically active population than registered voters, but a population for which there is good comparison

TABLE 1 Demographic, Socioeconomic, and Political Characteristics of the Sample

	2006 Hart Research Survey of Registered Voters		2006 CNN Exit Poll
	N	Percentage/median	Percentage/median
RACE			
White	624	78%	79%
Hispanic	62	8%	8%
Black	56	7%	10%
Asian	13	2%	2%
Other	49	6%	2%
GENDER			
Male	360	45%	49%
Female	444	55%	51%
INCOME			
Under $10,000	43	5%	—
$10,000–$20,000	76	10%	—
$20,000–$30,000	110	14%	—
$30,000–$40,000	104	13%	—
$40,000–$50,000	83	10%	—
$50,000–$75,000	126	16%	—
$75,000–$100,000	90	11%	—
More than $100,000	89	11%	—
Under $15,000	—	—	7%
$15,000–$30,000	—	—	12%
$30,000–$50,000	—	—	21%
$50,000–$75,000	—	—	22%
$75,000–$100,000	—	—	16%
$100,000–$150,000	—	—	13%
$150,000–$200,000	—	—	5%
$200,000 or more	—	—	5%
Median income	—	$40,000–$50,000	$50,000–$75,000
AGE			
18–29	100	12%	12%
30–44	171	21%	24%
45–59	248	31%	34%
60 and older	281	35%	29%
Refused	4	1%	—
Median age	—	50–54	45–59
PARTY IDENTIFICATION			
Democrat	305	38%	38%
Republican	239	30%	36%
Independent	260	32%	26%
EDUCATION			
Some high school or less	46	6%	3%
High school graduate	224	28%	21%
Some college	154	19%	31%
Vocational training or 2-year degree	64	8%	—
Bachelor's degree	165	21%	—
College graduate	—	—	27%
Postgraduate	128	16%	18%
Not sure/refused	23	3%	—

Note. Source: Author's analysis of 2006 Hart Research survey and 2006 CNN Voter Exit Poll.

data—indicate that the 2006 Hart poll is likely a representative sample. In 2006 voter exit polls, 79% of respondents were White, while 8% were Hispanic, 10% were Black, 2% were Asian, and 2% were "other." Women constituted 51% of the sample, while men made up 49%. In exit polls, the median annual income was between $50,000 and $75,000, and the median age was between 45 and 59. Of the voters, 38% supported the Democratic Party, 36% the Republican Party, and 26% considered themselves independent. Seventy-six percent of respondents completed at least some college.

The key questions in the 2006 Hart poll—those related to level of concern about retirement security, self-reliant values, and support for retirement policy reforms—are consistent with other polling on the subject. Level of concern about retirement security indicated in the Hart poll is in keeping with other polls from 2006 and, as we would expect, is slightly lower than polling from the current recession. The prevalence of self-reliant values and level of support for policy reforms closely mirrors that of polling from before and during the current recession.

In the Hart poll, the public's concern about retirement security is gauged by the following question: "How con dent are you that you will be able to retire with nancial security—would you say that you are very con dent, fairly con dent, just somewhat con dent, or not that con dent?" Similar to the ndings from other polls in 2006 (Newport, 2009; AEI Economic Insecurity Update, 2009; Helman et al., 2009; Bowman, 2008), about half the public said they were concerned about retirement, with 24% saying they were just somewhat con dent and 23% saying they were not that con - dent in their ability to retire with nancial security. Twenty-eight percent of respondents answered very con dent, and 24% answered that they were fairly con dent in their ability to retire.

Self-reliant values about retirement are determined by the following question: "Do you personally think that being able to retire with nancial security is a right that society should protect for all working people or a personal goal that people are responsible for achieving on their own?" Forty-seven percent of respondents said that retirement is a personal goal, while 39% said it is a right for all working people, and 11% of respondents answered that it is both a right and a responsibility—a choice that respondents had to volunteer on their own. These results are in keeping with other surveys showing that about half of Americans have strongly self-reliant views about retirement (AARP, 2005; Reynolds, Ridley, & Van Horn, 2005; National Institute on Retirement Security, 2009).

Initial support for policy reform is measured by a question that asks respondents whether they strongly favor, somewhat favor, somewhat oppose, or strongly oppose a proposal to "require companies to provide a pension plan that provides a guaranteed monthly income to their employees." This question was chosen for analysis because a government mandate that companies provide pensions is a type of policy solution that people with self-reliant values are likely to view as inconsistent with their values. The policy requires a signi cant new role for government and does not appear to be an incremental step that builds upon an existing program. Forty-three percent strongly favor the proposal and 36% somewhat favor it, while 8% somewhat oppose, 9% strongly oppose, and 4% were not sure. Other polling similarly nds that the public expresses high levels of initial support for retirement policy reforms, including government mandates on employers (National Institute on Retirement Security, 2009; Wright & Davies, 2007; *The Wall Street Journal*/NBC News, 1999; Yankelovich Inc., 2007).

Expectations about whether retirement policy reform will succeed is measured by a question that asks: "Would you say that the following is or is not a realistic national goal for retirement security: All working people should be able to retire at age 65 with a retirement income that is at least 70% of the income they were making before retirement." Forty-six percent of respondents said that national retirement security is a realistic goal, while 50% said it is not and 4% said they were not sure. It is not possible to compare directly the results of this question to other polling because publicly available polling does not probe such sentiments about retirement policy; however, the response is consistent with related polling. For example, polling on health care policy nds that Americans commonly think that reforms won't work (Americans for Health Care, 2005). Moreover, the question is a good measure of expectations. Asking whether providing retirement security for all Americans is realistic gets to the heart of people's expectations about a signi cant new governmental intervention in retirement policy. The question probes sentiment about an unfamiliar proposal and, as a result, is a good gauge of people's baseline expectations about the success of retirement policy reforms that require a new role for government.

Thus, the Hart survey provides good questions to study the in uence of self-interest and self-reliant values on retirement policy attitudes and is representative of the politically active population, making the survey ideal to use for our analysis.

RESULTS

Table 2 presents the results of an ordinary least squares regression testing the impact of self-interest and self-reliant values on support for retirement policy change. The dependent variable is the level of support for a government requirement that companies provide a pension plan to their employees that provides a guaranteed monthly income. The independent variables are self-reliant values, level of concern about retirement security, gender, education, income, age, and partisan identi cation.[4]

TABLE 2 Predicting Support for Requiring That Companies Provide Pensions, Results of a Linear Regression

	Expected Sign	β	SE	t	P
(Constant)		3.966	0.200	19.861	.000
Self-reliant values	−	−0.232	0.040	−5.758	.000
Concern about retirement security	+	0.054	0.024	2.284	.023
Age 30 to 39	−	−0.095	0.144	−0.661	.509
Age 40 to 49	−	−0.093	0.134	−0.689	.491
Age 50 to 59	−	−0.020	0.127	−0.160	.873
Age 60 to 69	−	−0.181	0.134	−1.357	.175
Age 70+	−	−0.049	0.137	−0.359	.720
Female	+	0.220	0.073	3.033	.003
Education	−	−0.053	0.027	−1.925	.055
Income	−	−0.012	0.020	−0.575	.566
Republican Party identification	−	−0.088	0.024	−3.640	.000

Note. $N = 654$.
Dependent variable = level of support for a policy to require that companies provide pensions.
Reference age category is 18 to 29.
Significance listed based on two-tailed test.
Source: Author's analysis of 2006 Hart Research survey.

The results of the regression indicate that, as expected, people with self-reliant values are much less likely to support mandatory pensions, a finding that is significant at the .001 level, while concern about retirement security increases support for requiring companies to provide pensions, a finding that is significant at the .05 level. Also as expected, women are more likely to support mandatory pensions, a result that is significant at the .01 level, while Republican Party identification and greater education are correlated with less support for the policy, results that are significant at the .001 and .1 levels, respectively. Income and age are not statistically significant, although their signs are in the predicted direction with increases in both correlated with less support for the policy. These results indicate that self-interest and self-reliant values affect support for retirement policy reforms in a similar manner as they affect support for other social welfare programs.

Moreover, the findings are quite robust. Alternative specifications produce virtually identical results. Running the same model with ordered probit (to account for the fact that the dependent variable is not perfectly continuous), self-reliant values continue to reduce policy support (significant at the .001 level), while concern about retirement security increases policy support, a finding that is significant at the .01 level. Women remain more likely to support mandatory pensions (significant at the .05 level), while Republican Party identification and higher levels of education continue to correlate with less support, significant at the .01 and .05 levels, respectively. Income and age are not statistically significant, although their signs are in the predicted directions. Similarly, adding or subtracting variables to the model

121

does not change the results. In such speci cations, running both ordinary least squares and ordered probit, all variables that were statistically significant remain so. Variables added to the model include concern for other workers' retirement, union membership, and attitudes toward employers.

While self-reliant values make it less likely that people will support policies to reform retirement, people with such values do commonly express support for policy reforms that require signi cant government intervention in the economy. For example, more than 60% of people with self-reliant values favor or strongly favor requiring that companies provide pensions. In short, many people are torn between their support for speci c retirement policy solutions and their general opposition to government intervention in the economy.

Whether people who are torn between their support for speci c retirement policy solutions and their general opposition to government intervention in the economy have low expectations, as theory suggests, is tested in Table 3, which displays the results of a logistic regression. The dependent variable in the regression is expectation about a policy for national retirement security. The independent variables are self-reliant values, concern about retirement security, age, gender, education, income, partisan identi cation, and the level of support for mandatory pensions. It is expected that opposition to mandating that companies provide pensions—a policy

TABLE 3 Predicting That Retirement Security Is a Realistic National Goal, Results of a Logistic Regression

	Expected sign	β	SE	P
Self-reliant values	−	−0.402	0.141	.005
Concern about retirement security		−0.027	0.081	.742
Support for mandatory pensions	+	0.269	0.134	.045
Age 30 to 39	−	−1.173	0.519	.024
Age 40 to 49	−	−0.083	0.459	.857
Age 50 to 59	−	−1.338	0.459	.004
Age 60 to 69	−	−0.419	0.453	.355
Age 70+	−	−0.151	0.450	.736
Female	+	−0.043	0.250	.864
Education	−	−0.105	0.094	.263
Income	−	−0.050	0.070	.474
Republican Party identi cation	−	−0.118	0.081	.148
Constant		1.338	0.853	.117

Note. N = 333.
Dependent variable = retirement security is a realistic national goal.
Reference age category is 18 to 29.
The N is smaller than the previous regression because the dependent variable was only asked of half the sample.
Signi cance listed based on two-tailed tests.
Source: Author's analysis of 2006 Hart Research survey.

reform that could help achieve national retirement security—is likely to make a person think the goal of achieving national retirement security is unrealistic.[5] Other control variables are expected to affect policy views as previously described.

As can be seen in the Table 3, people with self-reliant values, as expected, are far more likely than those without such values to have low expectations about a new national policy to ensure that all workers have secure retirements, a result that is signi cant at the .01 level. Importantly, self-interest does not impact expectations: Concern about retirement security is unrelated to whether retirement security is a realistic goal. Support for mandatory pensions increases people's expectations, as expected, a result that is signi cant at the .05 level. Age is negatively correlated with expectations, a result that is statistically signi cant for several age groups. Income, gender, education, and partisan identi cation do not have statistically significant effects. The signs on all of these non–statistically signi cant variables, except gender, are in the predicted directions.

The results presented in Table 3 are robust and remain virtually identical under a range of alternative speci cations. Similarly, adding or subtracting variables to the model does not change the results. In such speci cations, all variables that were statistically signi cant remain so. Variables added to the model include concern for other workers retirement, union membership, and attitudes toward employers.

Table 3 demonstrates that self-reliant values have a strong impact on expectations for retirement policy reform and have a far greater impact on expectations than does self-interest. As the data in the table help show, self-reliant values have a double impact on expectations: they directly lower expectations as well as affect policy preferences, which, in turn, affect expectations. In contrast, concern about retirement security does not directly impact expectations about the success of providing national retirement security. Concerns about retirement security only in uence policy views and therefore have an indirect impact on expectations. Thus, self-interest is subordinate to self-reliant values in lowering expectations about whether a policy will achieve its intended purpose.

In sum, the tension between self-interest and self-reliant values plays out in the initial level of support expressed for a policy. Here, these two forces pull in opposite directions. But expectations about the success of the policy are only directly in uenced by values, not self-interest. As a result, self-reliant values play a particularly prominent role in uencing attitudes about retirement policy.

DISCUSSION

The study indicates that concerns about retirement security lead to higher levels of support for retirement policy reform, including reforms that require signi cant government intervention in the economy such as a mandate that companies provide pensions. As a result, if people come to believe they have less retirement security, they will be more likely to support retirement reforms. But, if people perceive that their retirement prospects have improved, they may be less likely to support reforms.

While the public is very concerned about retirement security and these concerns have led to high levels of expressed support for retirement policy reform, as the study demonstrates, Americans generally have self-reliant values, and people with self-reliant values have lower expectations for the success of retirement policy reform. People think that policies that con ict with their self-reliant values will not achieve the intended goal. As a result, Americans are unlikely to think that retirement reforms requiring signi cant government intervention in the economy will work.

The political signi cance of these results is that public support for retirement policy reform should be considered relatively soft. Public support for retirement policy reform depends on being able to gain support from people with self-reliant values. Yet it will be dif cult to convince people with self-reliant values that retirement policy reforms will achieve their intended goals. People with self-reliant values—even those who support retirement policy reform—have low expectations for policy success. This nding is particularly signi cant because a plurality of those polled (44%) have self-reliant values and expressed initial support for retirement policy reform. This means that much of the support for retirement policy reform is inclined to believe that the reforms will not be successful. So even though retirement reform proposals that require signi cant government intervention may appear to have majority support, the public's attitudes about such policies are likely to be more negative.

Note that support for every type of retirement policy reform is not weakened to the same degree by self-reliant values. First, Americans think that some kinds of government programs are more consistent with their self-reliant values (Feldman & Zaller, 1992; Free & Cantril, 1968; Hasenfeld & Rafferty, 1989). Second, Americans like to use pragmatic arguments to justify their support for government interventions in the economy that are inconsistent with their self-reliant values (Feldman & Zaller, 1992). The basic sentiment that most Americans express when trying to justify their support for economic policy is that "even though people should get ahead on their own, they may still need help" (Feldman & Zaller, 1992, p. 285).

This suggests that retirement policy reforms that have strong contributory elements that reward individual initiative and are designed based on existing programs, with successful track records, are likely to enjoy higher levels of support. Such policies facilitate arguments that are likely to appeal to self-reliant Americans, namely, that such policies are pragmatic solutions to x important problems and are consistent with their self-reliant values. In contrast, policies that have less of a track record and less of a relationship between work and bene ts and thus must try to appeal to social rights are likely to face stronger opposition and are more susceptible to opposing arguments.

NOTES

1. The origins of this belief system are debated but often thought to be either the product of America's Protestant religious heritage or the result of the relative equality of conditions in which early settlers lived.

2. See for example, "A Better Stimulus Bill," *New York Times*, February 10, 2009; Peter Nicholas, "Obama hits the stimulus campaign trail," *Los Angeles Times*, February 10, 2009; Matt Welch, "The Cost of Doing Something," *Reason*, July 1, 2009.

3. Researchers have found that Americans are often torn between their general opposition to government and their support for speci c economic policies, although they have not focused on the impact of such con ict (Free & Cantril, 1968; Feldman & Zaller, 1992).

4. Age is operationalized as a series of dummy variables for different age groups because studies show that age has a nonlinear impact on economic policy views (Madland, 2008).

5. Note that the belief that retirement security is realistic is also likely to cause people to support the policy necessary to achieve the goal. As a result, policy views are both a dependent and independent variable. I chose to include level of support for mandatory pensions as an independent variable in the model for several reasons. My theory is that ideology shapes expectations directly, as well also indirectly through people's policy views. To rule out other explanations for the direct effect, I need to control for all other possible factors, including policy views. Similarly, in order to test the indirect effect, I need to include policy views in the model. In addition, when I run the model without policy views, all other results remain the same: all variables that are statistically signi cant remain so at the same levels, and statistically insigni cant variables do not become signi cant.

REFERENCES

AARP. (2005). *International Retirement Security Survey*. Washington, DC: AARP.

AEI Economic Insecurity Update. (2009). *Economic Insecurity Update: Americans' concerns about their jobs, personal finances, retirement, health costs, and more. American Enterprise Institute for Public Policy Research*. Retrieved October 25, 2009 from http://www.aei.org/docLib/AEI-Public-Opinion-Studies-Economic-2009.pdf.

Almeida, B., Kenneally, K., & Madland, D. (2008). *The new intersection on the road to retirement: Public pensions, economics, perceptions, politics, and interest groups*. Working Paper. University of Pennsylvania Wharton School Pension Research Council.

Americans for Health Care. (2005). *Health care poll*. Washington, DC: Center for American Progress. June.

Alvarez, R. M., & McCaffery, E. J. (2003). Are there sex differences in scal policy preferences? *Political Research Quarterly*, *56*(1), 5–17.

Blekesaune, M., & Quadagno, J. (2003). Public attitudes towards welfare state policies: A comparative analysis of 24 nations. *European Sociological Review*, *19*, 415–427.

Bowman, K. (2008). *Economic insecurity: Americans' concerns about their jobs, personal finances, retirement, health care, housing and more*. Washington, DC: American Enterprise Institute.

Chong, D., Citrin, J., & Conley, P. (2001). When self-interest matters. *Political Psychology, 22*(3), 541–570.

Cook, F. L., & Barrett, E. (1992). *Support for the American welfare state, the views of Congress and the public*. New York: Columbia University Press.

Doherty, D., Gerber, A., & Green, D. (2006). Personal income and attitudes toward redistribution: A study of lottery winners. *Political Psychology, 27*(3), 441–458.

Feldman, S., & Steenbergen, M. (2001). The humanitarian foundation of public support for social welfare. *American Journal of Political Science, 45*(3), 658–677.

Feldman, S., & Zaller, J. (1992). The political culture of ambivalence: Ideological responses to the welfare state. *American Journal of Political Science, 36*(1), 268–307.

Free, L., & Cantril, H. (1968). *The political beliefs of Americans, a study of public opinion*. New York: Simon and Schuster.

Gaventa, J. (1980). *Power and powerlessness, quiescence and rebellion in an Appalachian valley*. Chicago: University of Illinois Press.

Goss, K. (2006). *Disarmed: The missing movement for gun control in America*. Princeton, NJ: Princeton University Press.

Hart Research Associates. (2006). *Retirement security survey*. Washington, DC. July.

Hart Research Associates. (2009). *About us*. Retrieved September 10,2009, from http://www.hartresearch.com/about/

Hartz, L. (1955). *The liberal tradition in America: An interpretation of American political thought since the revolution*. New York: Harcourt Brace.

Hasenfeld, Y., & Rafferty, J. (1989). The determinants of public attitudes toward the welfare state. *Social Forces, 67*(4), 1027–1048.

Helman, R., Copeland, C., & VanDerhei, J. (2009). *The 2009 Retirement Confidence Survey: Economy drives confidence to record lows; many looking to work longer*. Washington, DC: Employee Bene t Research Institute.

Hochschild, J. L. (1981). *What's fair: American beliefs about distributive justice*. Cambridge, MA: Harvard University Press.

Jaeger, M. M. (2006). What makes people support public responsibility for welfare provision: Self-interest or political ideology? *Acta Sociologica, 49*(3), 321–338.

Jacobe, D. (2008). *Fewer Americans expect a comfortable retirement*. Washington, DC: Gallup.

Kingdon, J. W. (1995). *Agendas, alternatives, and public policies*. New York: HarperCollins College Publishers.

Lane, R. (2001). Self-reliance and empathy: The enemies of poverty and the poor. *Political Psychology, 22*(3), 473–492.

Madland, D. (2007). *A wink and a handshake: Why the collapse of the U.S. pension system has provoked little protest*. Graduate School of Arts and Science at Georgetown University. Unpublished dissertation.

Madland, D. (2008). *Progressive generation*. Washington, DC: Center for American Progress, May.

Madland, D., & Teixeira, R. (2009). *New progressive America: The millennial generation*. Washington, DC: Center for American Progress, May.

McClosky, H., & Zaller, J. (1984). *The American ethos, public attitudes towards capitalism and democracy*. Cambridge, MA: Harvard University Press.

Morin, R., & Taylor, P. (2009). *Different age groups, different recessions: Oldest are most sheltered*. Pew Research Center. Retrieved October 25, 2009 from http://pewsocialtrends.org/pubs/734/different-age-groups-different-recessions.

National Institute on Retirement Security. (2009). *Pensions & retirement security: A roadmap for policy makers*. National Institute on Retirement Security. Retrieved October 25, 2009 from http://www.nirsonline.org/storage/nirs/documents/nal_nirs_opinion_research_january_2009.pdf.

Newport, F. (2009). *Americans increasingly concerned about retirement income*. Gallup, April 20. Retrieved October 25, 2009 from http://www.gallup.com/poll/117703/americans-increasingly-concerned-retirement-income.aspx.

The New York Times. (2009). A better stimulus bill. February 10.

Page, B., & Shapiro, R. (1983). Effects of public opinion on policy. *American Political Science Review, 77*, 175–190.

Parsons, C., & Nicholas, P. (2009). Obama hits the stimulus campaign trail. *The Los Angeles Times*. February 10.

Pereira, J., & Van Ryzin, G. (1998). Understanding public support for time limits and other welfare reforms. *Policy Studies Journal, 26*(3), 398–418.

Ponza, M., Duncan, G., Concoran, M., & Groskind, F. (1989). The guns of autumn? Age differences in support for income transfers to the young and old. *Public Opinion Quarterly, 52*, 441–466.

Quadagno, J., & Street, D. (2005). Ideology and public policy, antistatism in American welfare state transformation. *Journal of Policy History, 17*(1), 52–71.

Reynolds, S., Ridley, N., & Van Horn, C. (2005). *A work-filled retirement: Workers' changing views on employment and leisure*. New Brunswick, NJ: Rutgers University, John J. Heldrich Center for Workforce Development.

Schlozman, K. L., & Verba, S. (1979). *Injury to insult: Unemployment, class, and political response*. Cambridge, MA: Harvard University Press.

Teixeira, R. (2006). *What the public really wants on health care*. Washington, DC: Center for American Progress.

Teixeira, R. (2008). *What the public really wants on retirement and social security*. Washington, DC: Center for American Progress.

The Wall Street Journal/NBC News. (1999). *Study #4096*. Washington, DC: Hart-Teeter.

Welch, M. (2009). The cost of doing something. *Reason*. July 1.

Weller, C. (2008). Testimony before the House Committee on Education and Labor, October 7.

Wright, W., & Davies, C. (2007). *Retirement Security Survey Report*. Washington, DC: AARP.

Yankelovich Inc. (2007). *American Worker Survey*. Washington, DC: The Rockefeller Foundation.

How to Supplement Social Security Fairly and Effectively

TERESA GHILARDUCCI, PhD

Bernard L. Schwartz Professor of Economic Policy Analysis, Department of Economics, The New School for Social Research, New York, New York, USA

Over the past 3 decades, the base upon which Americans obtain income for retirement has become increasingly tied to fluctuations in the financial markets. Because Social Security provides a small percentage of pre-retirement income in retirement, most of the nation's workers need a supplement to Social Security. This study demonstrates the failure of the 401(k) system and advances a bold, but realistic, solution to America's crumbling retirement system: guaranteed retirement accounts (GRAs), a universal government program that supplements Social Security by providing guaranteed rates of return, by locking up balances until retirement, and by mandating annuities at retirement—with survivor's benefits. The GRA plan is compared to other proposals, including President Obama's, which aims to expand the voluntary, commercial, individually directed account-based system.

INTRODUCTION

The nation's pension system cannot and does not provide retirement security for most Americans. This study presents a detailed pension reform proposal—the guaranteed retirement account (GRA)—to replace the current system. Over the past 3 decades, pensions have become more directly tied to nancial accounts because traditional pensions have been increasingly replaced by 401(k)-type accounts in which individuals invest funds in voluntary retirement accounts that are given preferential tax treatment. This " nancialization" of pensions in the United States is threatening people's retirement security because of many risks, including poor investment choices, high fees, and employees and employers not saving enough on a voluntary basis. This means that the boomer generation will replace less income in retirement than their grandparents and parents did: Boston College's National Income Security Index, which forecasts the likelihood retirees will have available 70% of their pre-retirement income—the minimum standard used for adequacy in retirement—and shows that 45% of Americans about to retire wouldn't reach that goal, whereas in 1992, only 32% were at risk of not reaching that standard (Munnell, Golub-Sass, & Webb, 2007). Much of the loss of pension security stems from inadequate coverage and account balances in de ned contribution (DC) accounts.

A GRA is a national system of individual accounts that supplements Social Security. Each year, employees would put at least 5% of their pay into their GRA, a government-backed savings account. Employers could pay part of that, if they wanted. The government would provide a $600 tax credit each year (indexed for in ation) to defray the employee's contributions. The money would earn an annual 3% interest after in ation and could be taken out only upon retirement as an annuity. It would be a safe place for people to save money, similar to what's already available for members of Congress and federal employees. The GRA is needed because our current system of pensions and 401(k)s is not working for most Americans. 401(k)s are not guaranteed, and pensions were designed when people worked for a single employer that was around for a lifetime, without bankruptcies. Mandated annuities eliminate adverse selection. People could opt out of GRAs if their pensions met GRA standards. GRAs would help low-wage workers and the self-employed in a way that the current system does not. GRAs are a government/private-sector partnership. The Social Security Administration would collect the money, and professional investors—overseen by independent and government-appointed trustees like any pension plan, for instance, like that for Federal Reserve employees—would invest the funds in a prudent portfolio. Only the U.S. government could invest worldwide in a diversi ed fund that pays a 3% real return for the long term with minimal fees.

This study reviews President Obama's proposals and critically analyzes the pitfalls of voluntary tax-incentivized, individual, commercial accounts. The next section describes GRAs in the short and long run. The political reality of Congress's mandating a forced savings tier onto Social Security is discussed along with an overview of international changes to pension systems.

PRESIDENT OBAMA'S PENSION PROPOSAL

President Obama has proposed to address inadequate retirement savings by expanding the number of Americans in individual retirement accounts (IRAs) and 401(k) plans, which are commercial, voluntary, individual accounts. The goal is to reach universal coverage and adequacy on an incremental basis. Ironically, the plan, devised by David John at the Heritage Foundation and Mark Iwry at Brookings Institution, was rst endorsed by the John McCain presidential campaign.

Obama presented his plan in the 2009–2010 budget,[1] proposing that employers who do not offer retirement plans enroll employees in a "direct-deposit IRA account." Employers without pension plans will put 3% of their workers' pay in 401(k)/IRA-type accounts. For households earning under $65,000, the federal government would match those savings up to $1,000 a year with a 50% tax credit. This progressive tax credit is aimed at increasing the savings rate for low- and middle-income workers. This plan might temporarily increase the IRA or 401(k) participation rate for low- and middle-income workers, but it might not, because workers can, at any time, opt out and withdraw their own funds and not participate.

Yet, by automatically enrolling 75 million Americans who do not have pension plans or 401(k) plans or IRAs, more people are likely to be in a plan, even if they can opt out. The president's proposal adds in tax credits that mitigate the regressivity of the tax subsidies (which take the form of tax expenditures—the value of taxes not collected because of a special provision in the tax code that favors certain activities). All retirement plans—de ned bene t (DB) pensions, 401(k) plans, IRAs, etc.—have special tax provisions: taxes on contributions and earnings are deferred until a person retires or withdraws income, which is usually when tax rates are lower than at the time of contributions and fund earnings. Therefore, tax deferrals are more valuable to people with high-income tax rates than to those with low or zero tax liability. On the other hand, a tax credit is given to any taxpayer, even those with incomes so low they do not pay federal income tax. The president's proposed tax credit means that all workers, not just those who itemize, will get some retirement savings subsidy, but Obama retains the current tax deduction, which means his plan is pricey—an extra $25 billion in tax expenditures (more below).

The Government Accountability Of ce (2009) reviewed the GRA plan and Obama's plan, along with two others, as well as approaches adopted by three European countries for their ability to address seven key pension system problems: lack of coverage, insuf cient contributions, risky investment returns, lack of portability, pre-retirement leakages, high fees, and the possibility of outliving retirement savings.

The Obama plan helps expand coverage but does not make it universal; it retains, but softens, the tax regressivity; investment returns are not guaranteed; and there are still pre-retirement leakages, high fees, and the longevity risk. In its favor, the president's plan maintains the portability of IRAs. The problems with any voluntary system that relies on tax incentives for participation (even if it is enhanced with an opt-out feature) and that is structured as individual commercial accounts are addressed in detail below.

Drawbacks to Voluntary, Tax-Incentivized, Individual, Commercial Retirement Accounts

Individuals and employers generally do not save enough in retirement plans: The typical contribution rate is 3% to 5%; experts recommend earners save 10% to 15% of every paycheck to accumulate enough to supplement Social Security. Early withdrawals are suspected to erode retirement savings (Vanguard Center for Retirement Research, 2009), although there is no systematic database following early withdrawals from DC accounts over time. The available evidence about withdrawals comes from various studies using different data sets. Two studies conclude that income shocks such as job loss and divorce increase the likelihood of withdrawals from 401(k) (Amromin & Smith, 2003).

Account managers track withdrawals. In 2007, before the 2008 nancial crises, over 50% of those eligible to take cash disbursements from their 401(k) accounts before retirement did so. "One-third of all Vanguard participants could have taken their account balance as a cash distribution because they had separated from service in the current or prior years. However, only 17% of these participants did so" (Vanguard Center for Retirement Research, 2008). After the nancial crises began in 2008, early withdrawals increased. More employers reported that they noticed more of their employees taking early withdrawals for hardship from their DC plans. The number of companies reporting more hardship withdrawals by their employees increased to 44% of respondents in April 2009 compared with 35% in February of 2009. Not only do early withdrawals from IRAs and 401(k) plans impose extra tax penalties on the accounts, the funds are not earning tax-deferred returns. Both factors erode pension savings.

Employer contributions are voluntary; employers voluntarily decide to sponsor 401(k)-type plans and also then decide whether to contribute. When many companies stopped their 401(k) contributions in late 2008 (*Watson Wyatt Insider*, 2009), many workers and the public, for the rst time, realized that employers were not required, beyond Social Security, to contribute to the pension and or retirement savings plans they sponsored.

There is no evidence that 401(k) plans grew because workers clamored for them at their jobs. Congress's liberalizing contributions into 401(k) plans encouraged their growth, which begs for another study about why Congress, year after year, raised contribution limits for 401(k)s while it imposed more stringent regulations on DB plans. In 2008, for people 50 years of age or older, this limit was $20,500, and for people younger than 50, the limit was $15,500. The total amount that can be contributed between employee and employer contributions is the smaller amount of 100% of the employee's compensation or $49,000 for 2009 (which is near the average wage for an American worker). Because they get the larger tax bene ts, higher-income people contribute more and more often to DC plans.

According to the Urban and Brookings Tax Policy Center, 76% of government subsidies for retirement accounts go to the top 20% of earners— those earning over $60,000 per year—and 50% of the tax expenditures go to the 6% of workers earning over $100,000 per year for contributions up to $20,000 per person per year (Toder, 2009). For more than 52% of Americans, tax units have earnings of less than $40,000. This is the way the current deduction works. A lawyer earning $200,000 makes a $1,000 contribution to his 401(k) plan and reduces income tax by $350. His receptionist, earning $20,000, makes the same $1,000 contribution (which is much less likely) and saves only $150 in taxes. This is not effective public policy: for all this mon- etary effort, the U.S. savings rates did not improve and pension coverage did not expand.

The lopsided distribution of tax breaks for pensions could have been predicted from the system's origins (Burman, Gale, Hall, & Orszag, 2004). 401(k) plans are named after the section of the tax code passed in 1978 intended to help high-income management employees save on a tax-favored basis. In the United States, provisions in the tax code that favor certain kinds of activities are signi cant sources of government subsidies to an activity, or in this case, the 401(k) system. Taxes not collected on pension contributions and earnings equal a fourth of annual Social Security contributions and, at over $114 billion, are perversely larger than household savings, totaling just over $102 billion (Bell, Carasso, & Steuerle, 2004).[2]

The typical 401(k) management fee easily erodes over 20% of account balances (Davis, 2008; Forman, 2007). But the ip side of high fees is high levels of revenue. Products in 401(k) plans and IRAs, mostly actively man- aged stock and bond mutual funds, added to the pro ts and growth of the nancial sector (Siedle, 2008).

Over $40 billion is paid in fees annually for 401(k) administration (Employee Bene t Research Institute, 2007).[3] Small differences in returns and in fees can add up over time to make large differences in workers' ultimate pension bene ts. A comprehensive study by Dutch and Canadian researchers Keith Ambachtsheer and Rob Bauer (2007) found that DB plans, where individuals do not direct the investment of their own accounts, earned a 2.66% higher return net of fees on equities than did retail mutual funds. The superiority in returns is due to both the reduction in fees for large insti- tutional investors and the fact that the trustees of pension plans are better investors than the employees. In Canada, the difference between the returns in DB plans and individual DC plans was even higher; the retail mutual funds earned 3.16% less. (These shortfalls are the averages for the 25-year period between 1980 and 2004 [Ambachtsheer & Bauer, 2007]). A 1% difference in net of fee returns over time can reduce accounts by 20% to 30%. The difference in costs is quite large because investing in retail funds means that investors pay for shareholder pro ts and aggressive advertising. Another way to understand the difference in cost managing DB plans and DC plans is that DB managers do not market to individuals at the retail level; they are chosen according to their performance by professional investors. Also, because employers chose the investment managers for their employees' 401(k) plans, they may have con icts of interest from relationships with the nancial rms who sponsor products in the rms' 401(k) plans for its workers (Jeszeck, 2009).

Individual-directed accounts are not well-managed by individuals; they make famous (Choi, Laibson, & Madrian, 2004) systematic investment mistakes: Behavioral economists note that investors chase winners and dump losers so that their dominant strategy is buying high and selling low. But even if workers were perfect investors and savers, one bad nancial downturn, like this one, can suddenly wipe out a third or more of savings. Furthermore, individuals often withdraw pension income in lump sums when changing jobs or retiring. This places retirees at risk for what a West Virginia administer of the teacher's fund calls "the red truck syndrome" (Levitz, 2008), referring to people making big durable purchases when receiving a large sum of money; it is one reason individuals may "outlive" their money if they have not pooled their accounts.

Guaranteed Retirement Accounts Could Be Available for Current 401(k) Holders to Swap

If Congress set up a GRA system this year, workers could voluntarily trade their 401(k) and 401(k)-type plan assets (perhaps valued at the average value of 2008) for GRAs (Ghilarducci, 2008). The value of the assets would be converted to credits for a pension to be paid at retirement. When the worker collects Social Security, the GRA will pay an in ation-adjusted annuity based on the accumulated funds. The credits will grow based on a 3% real rate of return; a 3% interest rate adjusted for a 3% in ation rate would pay 6%. The GRA accounts are similar to existing plans available to some American workers already. GRAs are essentially a "cash balance account"—a DB plan with DC but guaranteed interest rates. GRAs are somewhat modeled after the TIAA (Teachers Insurance and Annuity Association) portion of the college professors' pension plan TIAA-CREF.

How would the swap of GRAs for a 401(k) plan work? Take a 55-year-old who had $50,000 in his 401(k) account in August. He can swap out the $50,000 for a guarantee of $500 per month.[4]

One salubrious macroeconomic consequence of a widespread conversion to guaranteed accounts from 401(k) plans would be to diminish the nancial anxiety and consumer spending withholding that came from the negative wealth shock of the 2009 recession. Secure pensions could help restore aggregate demand.

GRAs in the Long Term

Over the longer term, GRAs could compete effectively with current DC plans, the majority of which are 401(k)s and IRAs. In GRAs, workers and employers each contribute 2.5% of salary in individual accounts managed by the Social Security Administration and a newly created investment board. Government employees, appointed by the president and Congress, invest the money in bond and equity markets, and these trustees are accountable to Congress, as is the case in Canada. The government would guarantee an annual investment return of 3% beyond in ation. The government is the only entity with a long enough time horizon to guarantee an indexed return and withstand the ups and downs of the nancial markets. Since the historical rate of return is closer to 6%, excess returns could be distributed periodically as dividends. Unlike 401(k) accounts, GRAs would have no investment risk, and their administrative costs would be minimal because the contributions would be pooled and run by professionals on a not-for-pro t basis. The funds are mandated and guaranteed so there is no advertising. The private investment industry will still have a role: the government trustees would hire for-pro t brokers and nancial institutions to invest the funds.

Retirement Income Security Promises of GRAs

All workers, not just those working for rms that sponsor voluntary retirement plans, would have IRAs supplementing their Social Security bene ts funded by a $600 contribution from the government, plus worker and employer contributions. People would contribute constantly, not just when they are lucky enough to have three characteristics: working for a rm with a plan, being eligible for the plan, and participating in the plan. The accumulations from consistent 5%-of-pay-contributions, earning a 3% real rate of return and being paid as an indexed-annuity at retirement means that, with Social Security, the average worker will achieve a secure 71% replacement rate and the National Retirement Risk Index would show very few at risk of achieving subpar replacement rates.

The average earner, making $39,000 per year, would accumulate $172,300 in a GRA and get an annuity of $5,800 per year. This is 30% of pre-retirement income. Combined with the Social Security replacement rate of 41%, the average earner would achieve a total replacement rate of 71%! A high earner (in this example with an annual income of $62,000), because she gets a lower Social Security bene t relative to income, would get a 64% replacement rate, and the low earner ($17,000 per year) would get a much needed higher replacement rate of 86% (Ghilarducci, 2007).

Therefore, the United States would have a universal second tier of retirement income support that would be advance-funded on top of the pay-as-you-go Social Security system. By rearranging the tax code, the United States can obtain universal coverage and not spend any more than the treasury is spending now. The GRA plan pays for itself—it will not increase the federal de cit or require a tax increase—by eliminating all tax deductions for contributions to 401(k) plans. If contributions up to $5,000 a year were allowed, the credit could be reduced to $400 and the effect would still be revenue-neutral. Mandating contributions in a GRA means that all workers steadily accumulate assets to fund their golden years with the federal government's help, and the government—the only institution that can—takes on longevity, investment, nancial, and in ation risk. The hard-to-see indirect subsidy for retirement savings would turn into a tax credit and retirement contribution of $600 for everyone and actually raise national savings rates and secure Americans' retirement futures.

Despite some clear gains in terms of coverage, ef ciency, and effectiveness, there is opposition to GRAs.

Resistance to the GRA Plan

There are two key criticisms of the GRA plan: the guarantee might pose an expensive entitlement for the federal government to fund over time, and it will reduce the size of the mutual fund industry. The rst is a serious public policy issue; the second is not.

The federal government promises to provide a 3% real return rate; however, there are key provisions in the plan that would allow the rate to uctuate depending on the real growth rate in the economy. In fact, the 3% real return guarantee was selected to correlate roughly with the growth rate in real gross domestic product (GDP), in the productive base of the economy, not to uctuations in the stock market. The intention is that the GRA board of trustees, under extenuating circumstances and after extensive hearings and consideration, could vary the guarantee rate if the economy does much better than grow at 3% real for an extended period of time or suffers long-term slower growth. The principle behind benchmarking the rate of return to the GDP real growth rate is that workers who save should earn a rate of return that re ects the talents, efforts, and resources of the same cohort of workers. A 3% real rate of return locked in stone would be in exible and cause some risk to the treasury if GDP was considerably lower for long periods of time (Munnell, Golub-Sass, Kopke, & Webb, 2009). Independent analyses of the performance of nancial markets and professionally run pension funds nd that the risk that the federal government will underperform a 3% rate of return for sustained periods of time to be low. But a low risk may be too high; this is a political question, not an economic one. There are many ways to construct a guarantee around a band of returns, and the details should be left to professionals who manage guarantees in other types of cash balance funds here and abroad.

The second source of resistance for a public option, an alternative to 401(k) plans, comes from the commercial mutual fund industry that enjoys advantages from the current system. Above, I documented the pro tability of the 401(k) design for retail mutual fund rms. The loss in fee income has created a strong lobbying force against the GRA.[5]

Some employers may be the third source of opposition. They may enjoy the advantages that the current 401(k) system provides to pay workers less than they think they are earning. A study of 700 rms over 17 years found that if a rm adopted a 401(k), it lowered pension expenses by 3.5% to 5% and workers did not complain (Ghilarducci & Sun, 2006). Since 401(k) plans are voluntary, about 20% of workers who can avoid contributing do so and "leave money on the table" by not accepting the employer match. As a result, employers' contributions are 26% lower than they would be if everyone participated (Munnell & Sundén, 2004).[6]

Given this opposition, the next section explores whether Congress would ever implement a mandated individual account tier to Social Security.

Would Congress Ever Mandate Savings?

Most of the proposals for pension reform do not mandate savings (Mensah & Perun, 2007). The major advantages of a mandate are that workers would not have to be enticed to save by expensive tax breaks or the ability to withdraw funds at any time. There may be untapped support for mandated savings.

Surveys show that fewer than 50% of people think they will live comfortably in retirement, and at the same time, they show that workers feel personally responsible to supplement their Social Security bene ts (Madland, 2008). Despite feeling responsible, they want the government to help. In 2006, HSBC Bank asked 21,000 workers in 20 nations what their governments should do about the expense of aging societies (HSBC Bank, 2007). On average, respondents preferred compulsory savings to any other policy. A third of Americans responding to the survey wanted the government to force them to save more for retirement; far fewer, 16%, would support a tax increase; and only 9% wanted the government to reduce bene ts. In October 2007, a whopping 91% of respondents to a *Wall Street Journal* poll felt that the government should do something to secure retirement, and 41% said they were not hearing enough from the presidential candidates about retirement income issues (Bright, 2009).

Other experts and reforms in other countries support the notion that mandatory savings can be politically feasible. Adam Carasso and Jonathan Barry Forman (2007) have proposed a universal pension system requiring an annual employer contribution of 3% of earnings. Alicia Munnell (2009) also proposes a mandatory tier of pension saving.

In July 1, 2007, New Zealanders instituted the KiwiSaver program, a subsidized DC plan offered by private-sector providers. New labor force entrants in permanent positions, aged 18 or older, are automatically enrolled, but they can opt out. Employees contribute either 4% or 8% of gross earnings. Beginning April 1, 2008, all employers are required to contribute 1% of gross earnings in 2008, increasing 1% each year to 4% in 2011. Employers receive a tax credit of up to NZ $20 (about US $16) per week per employee. Workers who contribute receive a tax credit of up to NZ $1,040 (about US $836) a year, deposited directly into their KiwiSaver accounts (Kritzer, 2008).[7] Obama's proposal is similar to the KiwiSaver only in that employees can opt out, but it is not similar because employers must contribute.

On the other hand, employees cannot opt out of the Australian pension system, which is funded by 9% compulsory employer contributions. The system supplements the non-contributory basic pension paid at age 65 to all Australian residents with assets or income below a threshold, which provides a at payment amount pegged at about 25% of the median wage. The Australian system is similar to the GRA in that coverage is mandatory, but the GRA pays out in annuities and the return is guaranteed.

In the Netherlands, the new pension plan is like the GRA in that it is a hybrid plan as well—the collective de ned contribution plan. The employer must abide by a xed contribution rate, and there are no additional obligations if the plan becomes underfunded. The fund uses the contributions to grant a conditional career-average bene t: investment risk falls on the plan and the employees and pensioners. In the Dutch system, there are no individual accounts, and employees do not make investment choices: The funds are pooled and professionally managed. This is similar to the GRA.

CONCLUSION

After World War II and up to the 1980s, the U.S. retirement system was based on institutions established in the Great Depression and during World War II—Social Security and the employer voluntary provision of DB pensions and health insurance. By 2009, in the United States, almost all American retirees receive income from Social Security—about half from a middle tier of employer pensions, including 401(k)s—and the top 20% receive income from personal savings. The American retirement system is not a three-legged stool composed of equal parts: Social Security, employment-based pension plans, and personal wealth. The appropriate image is a pyramid, like the nutritional food pyramid, with Social Security at the base, the employer system in the middle, and personal wealth at the top. It is the top two layers that are crumbling.

Savings rates have long been low, while the collapse of the housing market has demolished a critical pillar of wealth for many households. Meanwhile, half of all private-sector workers do not have access to pension plans or 401(k) plans at work. Many workers who are offered such plans fail to participate, and importantly, when they do participate, they do not save enough; they withdraw the funds before retirement and they are exposed to risks in the stock market as well as the risk of outliving their money when they retire. Financial markets are risky, and tens of millions of older Americans who do have 401(k) plans have recently seen those investments wiped out in a very short time, changing their retirement and work plans forever.

Just as the last Great Depression reordered the nancial institutions that secured pensions, the 2009 nancial crises eroded the non–Social Security layers of the pension system. Therefore, the crises may provide the opportunity to create a supplement to Social Security. This new layer of pension income could come from an advance-funded, professionally managed system—the GRA.

NOTES

1. Obama's plan is based on the proposal by David John from the Heritage Foundation and Mark Iwry from the Retirement Security Project sponsored by the Hamilton Project. The proposal is explained most recently in their testimony to the U.S. Senate (John & Iwry, 2008). "We introduced this in 2006. . . . The McCain campaign endorsed the proposal. My colleague Mark Iwry advised the Obama campaign and they also endorsed it. It was the same identical proposal. We felt pretty good going into the November elections. Since then, the Obama administration included the automatic [IRA] in the budget, and they have explicitly endorsed the proposal" (Pichardo-Allison, 2009, p. 1).

2. Bell et al., (2004): In an unpublished memo, dated Feb. 19, 2009, to the House Labor and Education subcommittee. I used multiple regression methodology and two sources of data, The Of ce of Management and Budget and the Joint Congressional Committee on Taxation, to nd that tax expenditures have a negative to no effect on increasing. The negative effect makes sense if savers are target savers; in other words, savers have a savings goal and the government subsidy helps them get there without reducing their current spending. Memo available from the author.

3. There is $2.7 trillion in 401(k) assets (Employee Bene t Research Institute, 2007). The average fee is over $700 per year and average fees are 1.5% of assets, which equals $40.5 billion.

4. This is what the annuity would pay at a 3% in ation rate and a 3% real return.

5. http://www. nancialweek.com/article/20081102/REG/311039998/O/ISSUEINDEX

6. Calculations are made using information from Munnell and Sundén (2004). The data on participation rates, average contribution levels by earnings, and the distribution of employees by earnings are calculated from the current population survey (2003) to make the $3 billion estimate. The average savings per worker is derived from the $156 estimate in Choi, Laibson, and Madrian (2005). They calculated, from their sample of more than 800 employees in one rm, that the employer saved over $250 per older worker who did not participate in the 401(k) even when they were eligible. Fidelity's (2004) annual report documents employers' match behavior (Schwab, 2010).

7. Until March 2011, if both the employer and the employee agree, they may divide the employee's contribution. The government provides two other subsidies: a one-time tax-free payment of NZ $1,000 (about US $804) to each account after it receives the rst contribution and a NZ $40 (about US $32) annual fee subsidy to each account holder (Kritzer, 2008).

REFERENCES

Ambachtsheer, K., & Bauer, R. (2007). Losing ground. *Canadian Investment Review*; Spring, *20*(1), 8–14.

Amromin, G., & Smith, P. (2003). What explains early withdrawals from retirement accounts? Evidence from a panel of Taxpayers. *National Tax Journal*, September, 595–612.

Bell, E., Carasso, A., & Steuerle, C. E. (2009). *Retirement savings incentives and personal savings, tax notes, December 20*. Unpublished memo, dated Feb. 19, 2009, to the House Labor and Education Committee.

Bright, B., (2009). *Americans see a dim outlook for social security.* Retrieved March 18, 2010 from http://online.wsj.com/public/article_print/SB119500312722492114.html.

Burman, L. E., Gale, W. G., Hall, M., & Orszag, P. R. (2004). *Distributional effects of defined contribution plans and individual retirement accounts.* Washington, DC: Urban-Brookings Tax Policy Center.

Carasso, A., & Forman, J. B. (2007). *Tax considerations in a universal pension system. Discussion Paper No. 28.* Washington, DC: Urban-Brookings Tax Policy Center.

Choi, J. J., Laibson, D. I., & Madrian, B. C. (2004). *Plan design and 401(k) savings outcomes. Working Paper 10486.* Cambridge, MA: National Bureau of Economic Research.

Choi, J. J., Laibson, D. I., & Madrian, B. C. (2005). *$100 bills on the sidewalk: Suboptimal investment in 401(K) plans. Working Paper, Vol. w 11554.* Cambridge, MA: National Bureau of Economic Research.

Davis, D. A. (2008). How much is enough? Giving duciaries and participants adequate information about plan expenses. *Marshall Law Review, 41*, 1005.

Employee Bene t Research Institute. (2007). *401(k) plan asset allocation, account balances, and loan activity: An information sheet from the Employee Benefit Research Institute (EBRI).* Retrieved March 18, 2010 from www.ebri.org/pdf/InfSheet.QDIA.23Oct07.Final.pdf.

Forman, J. B. (2007). The future of 401(k) plan fees. In A. D. Lurie, (Ed.), *New York University Review of Employee Benefits and Compensation*, 9–18.

Government Accountability Of ce. (2009). *Alternative approaches could address retirement risks faced by workers but pose trade-offs.* Retrieved March 18, 2010 from http://www.gao.gov/new.items/d09642.pdf.

Ghilarducci, T. (2008). *When I'm sixty-four: The plot against pensions and the plan to save them.* Princeton, NJ: Princeton University Press.

Ghilarducci, T. (2007). *Guarantee retirement account: Toward retirement income security.* Retrieved March 18, 2010 from http://www.sharedprosperity.org/bp204.html.

Ghilarducci, T., & Sun, W. (2006). How de ned contribution plans and 401(k)s affect employer pension costs: 1981–1998. *Journal of Pension Economics and Finance, 5*(2), 175–196.

HSBC Bank. (2007). *How should governments finance ageing populations?* Retrieved March 18, 2010 from http://www.hsbc.com/1/PA_1_1_S5/content/assets/retirement/2005_for_report.pdf.

HSBC. (2006). *The future of retirement: What people want*. Retrieved February 11, 2009, from http://hsbc.com/1/2/newsroom/news/2006/hsbc_publishes_future_of_retirement_what_the_world_wants#top.

Jeszeck, C. A. (2009). *Testimony before the Subcommittee on Health, Employment, Labor, and Pensions, Education and Labor Committee, House of Representatives: Private pensions—conflicts of interest can affect defined benefit and defined contribution plans*. March 24.

John, D. C., & Iwry, J. M. (2008). *Strategies to reduce leakage in 401(k)s and expand saving through automatic IRAs: Testimony before the special committee on aging*. Hearing on Protecting and Strengthening Retirement Savings, July 16.

Kritzer, B. E. (2008). *KiwiSaver: New Zealand's new subsidized retirement savings plans*. Division of Program Studies, Of ce of Research, Evaluation, and Statistics, Of ce of Retirement and Disability Policy, Social Security Administration.

Levitz, J. (2008). Teachers in West Virginia offer a valuable lesson for what not to do. *Wall Street Journal*, August 4.

Madland, D. (2008). *Reforming retirement: What the public thinks*. Georgetown University Conference on "The Future of Retirement Security," October 3.

Mensah, L., & Perun, P. J. (2007). *Savings for life: A pathway to financial security for all Americans*. Retrieved March 18, 2010 from http://ssrn.com/abstract=982931.

Munnell, A. H. (2009). *The financial crisis and restoring retirement security*. Testimony before the Committee on Education and Labor, U.S. House of Representatives, February 24. Retrieved March 18, 2010 from http://edlabor.house.gov/documents/111/pdf/testimony/20090224AliciaMunnellTestimony.pdf.

Munnell, A. H., Golub-Sass, F., & Webb, A. (2007). *What moves the National Retirement Risk Index? A look back and an update. Issue in Brief, 7-1*. Chestnut Hill, MA: Center for Retirement Research at Boston College.

Munnell, A. H., Golub-Sass, F., Kopcke, R. W., & Webb, A. (2009). *What does it cost to guarantee returns? Issue Brief 9-4*. Chestnut Hill, MA: Center for Retirement Research at Boston College.

Munnell, A. H., & Sundén, A. (2004). *Coming up short: The challenge of 401(k) plans*. Washington, DC: Brookings Institution Press.

Pichardo-Allison, R. (2009). *A change to retirement savings we need. Global Pensions*. Retrieved October 31, 2009, from http://www.globalpensions.com/global-pensions/interview/1496093/a-change-retirement-services-need.

Schwab. (2010). *Charles Schwab releases data on employer and worker 401(k) behavior*. Retrieved March 18, 2010 from http://www.businesswire.com/portal/site/schwab/index.jsp?ndmViewId=news_views&ndmCon gId=1016332&newsId=2009061005397&newsLang=en

Siedle, E. (2008). *Secrets of the 401k industry: How employers and mutual fund advisers prospered as workers' dreams of retirement security evaporated. Benchmark Financial Services, Inc.* Retrieved May 20, 2009, http://www.benchmarkalert.com/Secrets%20of%20the%20401k%20Industry.pdf.

Toder, E. J., Harris, B. H., & Lim, K. (2009). *Distributional effects of tax expenditures. Tax Policy Center, Urban Institute and Brookings Institution*. Retrieved March 18, 2010 2009, from http://www.newschool.edu/cepa/publications/Distributional%20effects%20of%20tax%20expenditures%20 nal.pdf.

Vanguard Center for Retirement Research. (2008). *How America saves 2008: A report on Vanguard 2007 defined contribution plan data.* Retrieved March 18, 2010 from https://advisors.vanguard.com/VGApp/iip/site/advisor/researchcommentary/research/article?File=IWE_ResearchHowAmericaSaves08.

Vanguard Center for Retirement Research. (2009). *2008 hardship withdrawals.* Valley Forge, PA: Vanguard.

Watson Wyatt Insider. (2009). *Economic crisis prompts many companies to suspend contributions to employee savings plans.* Retrieved March 18, 2010 from http://www.watsonwyatt.com/us/pubs/insider/showarticle.asp?ArticleID=21034.

Index

INDEX

Printed and bound by CPI Group (UK) Ltd, Croydon, CR0 4YY

01/11/2024

01782608-0001